THIS CLIMBING GAME

AN ANTHOLOGY OF MOUNTAIN HUMOUR

Compiled by Walt Unsworth

VIKING

VIKING
Penguin Books Ltd, Harmondsworth, Middlesex, England
Viking Penguin Inc, 40 West 23rd Street, New York, New York 10010, U.S.A.
Penguin Books Australia Ltd, Ringwood, Victoria, Australia
Penguin Books Canada Ltd, 2801 John Street, Markham, Ontario Canada L3R 1B4
Penguin Books (N.Z.) Ltd, 182–190 Wairau Road, Auckland 10, New Zealand

This collection first published 1984

Set in VIP Palatino
Typeset, printed and bound in Great Britain by
Hazell Watson & Viney Limited,
Member of the BPCC Group,
Aylesbury, Bucks

BRITISH LIBRARY CATALOGUING IN PUBLICATION DATA

This climbing game.
  1. Mountaineering – Anecdotes, facetiae,
  satire, etc.
  I. Unsworth, Walt
  796.5'22   GV200

ISBN 0-670-80057-0

Contents

III. Offside

Preface

The articles, stories and poems which make up this anthology have been quarried from the vast scree slopes of mountain literature. They are among the lighter detritus, telling as much about human follies and foibles as they do about high adventure, which is why they should appeal to climber and non-climber alike. The misfortunes of others appeal to us all!

Readers seeking a Heavy Message should put the book down at once because they'll find none here. The purpose is to amuse and entertain, nothing more. If it whiles away a tedious train journey or fills in the hours of boredom at a strikebound Heathrow, and leaves the reader feeling more cheerful, then it will have done its job.

Walt Unsworth,
Harmony Hall,
Milnthorpe,
Cumbria

Acknowledgements

My thanks are due to the following for pieces used in the book: Victor Gollancz Ltd for extracts from Tom Patey's *One Man's Mountain*; Robert Schultheis for *Khyber Taxi* and *Chang*; Kevin Fitzgerald for *I'm a Sick Man, Fitzgerald*; A. G. Cram, Editor of the FRCC Journal, for *The Trippercrock*; Brigadier D. H. Davis for extracts from H. W. Tilman's *Mount Everest, 1938*; Showell Styles for *The Ascent of F#*, *The Climber's Clementine* and *The Ballad of Idwal Slabs*; Peter Graves for *A Day with the Angel*; Prof. G. J. F. Dutton for *Chalking It Up*; John Barry for *It's an Ill Wind*; John Barry and Diadem Ltd for *Raven's with the Great Man* from *Cold Climbs*; Rick Ayres for *Further Notes on Manwatching*; H. R. C. Carr for an extract from *A Climber's Guide to Snowdon*; I. G. McNaught Davis for *Mac the Belly Talks to Cassius Bonafide*; Bill Howarth for *Wildmen*; J. M. Dent & Sons Ltd for the extract from Janet Adam Smith's *Mountain Holidays*; Guy Waterman for *The Gearfreak Caper*; Macdonald & Co. for the extract from W. E. Bowman's *The Ascent of Rum Doodle*; Mike Thompson for *Out with the Boys Again*; S. Russell Jones for *In Nepal, Mission Aborted* and *Cautionary Epigrams*; Mrs E. Wilson for extracts from George Abraham's *Modern Mountaineering* and *British Mountain Climbs*; Rev. S. Z. Edwards for Menlove Edwards's *A Great Effort* and extracts from *Tryfan Group* and *Cwm Idwal Group*; D. Knighton, A. Phizacklea and Cicerone Press for the extract from *Rock Climbs, Lancashire and the North West*; Mrs G. Sutton for *The Man Who Broke the Needle* from Graham Sutton's *Fell Days*.

Every effort was made to contact the authors of the various extracts or their literary heirs, but this was not always possible: I apologize for any apparent discourtesy.

My thanks are also due to the many mountaineering friends who offered advice and encouragement during the preparation of the anthology, and especially to Ivan Cumberpatch, whose illustrations are, as always, a delight.

Walt Unsworth

Introduction

The chief difference between football and climbing is that in the latter sport you can get kicked into touch permanently. The rules of the game are such that a loser seldom gets a return fixture. Everything else is a draw – there are no outright winners, because, as the great George Mallory once said, 'What have we conquered?' and came up with the answer: 'Nothing but ourselves.' The mountain is always there, win or lose.

Given such a situation an outsider might be forgiven for thinking that climbing is a pretty serious business and hardly a cause for laughter; but he would be quite wrong. It is precisely *because* it is a serious business that its participants have a highly developed sense of humour, even in the most dangerous situations. A typical story concerns a companion of Frank Smythe who was almost killed by an avalanche: 'Let's get back to terra firma,' he said. 'More firmer and less terror.'

No doubt the psychologists would attribute this to a form of defence mechanism, and they may be right; but I think it goes beyond that. When you have fallen twenty feet and been saved from certain death by a nylon rope and a trusted friend, or when you have crouched behind a boulder in the Alps whilst God hurled rocks down the mountain at you, you begin to get a different perspective on life. There is certainly an awareness of the tenuous hold we have on it, which frequently leads young climbers to follow the philosophy laid down by Omar Khayyám. After all, who knows when the hand of the Potter might shake?

The most obvious and everyday expression of mountain humour is to be found in the names which climbers give to their routes. In the pioneering days climbs were generally named after the crag, or sometimes the climber, so that you got routes like Bowfell Buttress in Langdale or Jones's Route on Scafell, but this didn't last long. On Bowfell Buttress is Sinister Slabs – a route which is both *harder and to the left* of the original. Not far away there is a famous climb called Kipling's Groove – because it is 'ruddy 'ard'. It is a simple humour in which alliteration, puns and pure corn all play a part. If some boring old climber puts up two climbs which he calls Route 1 and Route 2 and you put up a new climb in between them, what else can you call it but Route 1·5? If the name is puzzling, as it sometimes seems, there's generally a reason for it to be found somewhere – for example, take the climb called Solomon, on Lliwedd, which is inexplicable until you know that it bisects a rock feature known as the Quartz Babe.

Unfortunately there has been a tendency in recent years for names to appear which have neither wit nor decency and have been labelled as guidebook graffiti. There is, thank goodness, a growing resentment at this flouting of tradition.

Not all climbers have a sense of humour, of course – I know one or two quite eminent mountaineers who are good chaps but wouldn't recognize a joke if it got up and bit them. With one of these I was once crossing a high and lonely Alpine pass and in my rucksack I had some hard-boiled eggs, about a week old. It struck me that if we were to construct a stone nest and place the eggs in it, the next traveller to pass that way might well think he had discovered the last site of the Great Auk – a discovery which, if reported, would astonish the scientific world. The possibilities seemed endless! But my companion vetoed the plan. He felt he might need the eggs at a later date.

In earlier times innocent fun sometimes caused tremendous rows. When Leslie Stephen, the great Victorian pioneer, made fun of the pseudo-scientific attitude to mountaineering adopted by some of his contemporaries, Professor Tyndall resigned from the Alpine Club in a rage. Stephen was Virginia Woolf's father, so I suppose he needed a sense of humour.

But by and large the pioneers liked a chuckle. Even the great Edward Whymper – by no means a fun person – could see the humour in Old Semiond's remark, 'Ah! As to fleas, I don't pretend to be different to anybody else – I have them.'

When the pioneers of climbing wrote about their adventures – and most of them did – they did so with appropriate Victorian modesty. Their expeditions were usually arduous or dangerous, or both, but a writing technique had to be devised which, whilst it left the reader in no doubt about the desperate adventures undertaken by the author, didn't actually say so in as many words. This was all very well, but as times changed the Stiff Upper Lip style began to look ridiculous, perhaps because it was taken up so avidly by boys' adventure comics.

The ultimate in this type of writing came from Frederick Burlingham, who, in 1914, wrote a textbook called *How To Become An Alpinist*, and included a chapter entitled *How To Get Killed In The Alps*: '. . . the three Englishmen and Tairraz went to destruction,' he wrote. 'Tairraz screamed, but, like Englishmen, the others met their doom without a word of exclamation.' Poor old Burlingham – his book became an instant hoot. A critic suggested that only the omission of the word 'not' from the title prevented it from becoming the perfect textbook.

Climbers quickly realized that absurdity could be avoided yet modesty preserved by a cloak of light-hearted banter. Even the most hazardous situations could be treated as a huge joke, and so there evolved what might be termed the Fortescue Was Neatly Fielded school, in which the reader was left under no illusions as to what would have happened to poor Fortescue had he *not* been neatly fielded, but had continued his downwards flight-path another three hundred feet to the bottom of the crag.

The beauty of this sort of humour was that it not only preserved modesty but actually emphasized the real dangers so lightly described. Everybody understood the rules and liked them, so that this became one of the most enduring forms of mountain writing, and examples can be gleaned from every period, right up to the present. John Barry's *Raven's with the Great Man* is a typical modern example.

Sometimes it seems to be almost *too* pervasive. It even creeps into guidebooks: 'I don't trust English guidebooks,' an American climber recently wrote. 'If they say something is just a scramble I know I'm going to be stretched to the limit.' In a guide to a Welsh crag, Menlove Edwards wrote: 'It may be considered safe for humanity – nobody has been killed there for years.'

Edwards was a psychiatrist whose theories took him into deep and murky waters from which ultimately he found no escape except in suicide, and his humour was often pointed at some mental frailty of the climber, as in *A Great Effort*. The tendency of the best of later writers has been to poke fun at mountain shibboleths like massive Himalayan expeditions or the ever more expensive and technical equipment coming on to the market – Guy Waterman's *Gearfreak Caper* is a witty send-up of the latter, disguised as a Nero Wolfe detective story. Pure satire, where the target is unmistakable and the knife sharp, has never been better done than in the series of short pieces Ian McNaught Davis wrote for *Mountain* magazine in the early seventies, of which *Mac the Belly Talks to Cassius Bonafide* is a superb example.

Undoubtedly the most popular mountain humorist of recent years was Tom Patey, a Scottish doctor tragically killed in an abseiling accident. Patey's writings included songs and verse as well as articles and much of it was gathered together in a posthumous collection called *One Man's Mountains*. In *A Short Walk with Whillans*, he teams up with a man who has become a legend in his own lifetime and who is himself an acknowledged master of wit – though of the spoken rather than the written kind. Stories about Don Whillans abound in climbing circles and he is unquestionably the greatest folk-hero the sport has ever seen. He comes to the fore again in the delightful piece by Mike Thompson called *Out with the Boys Again* – an essay which Bonington is said to have regarded as distinctly subversive!

Humorous verse was popular in mountaineering journals of yesteryear, but apart from Tom Patey, the only recent practitioner of note is Selwyn Russell Jones, whose poems often are more thought-provoking than many so-called 'serious' pieces. His poem *In Nepal* succinctly and humorously raises the spectre of what tourism might do to that beautiful country. On the other hand, *The Ballad of Idwal Slabs* by Showell Styles is a much-loved piece of pure entertainment written, so the author assured me, in a few minutes before the club dinner at which it was first recited.

In mountain literature fiction has never played a strong part, perhaps because the real live subject is more than adequate. It is one field of human endeavour in which truth very often is stranger than fiction: there are quite a few mountaineering incidents which, though they actually happened, are so bizarre that no fiction writer would dare to invent them. My own piece *But I Don't Want to be Rescued* is a case in point: a true tale that still goes the round of the Fort William bars when talk is of mountain rescue.

Nevertheless, there are some stories that have become classics over the years, especially C. E. Montague's *In Hanging Garden Gully* and Graham Sutton's *The Man Who Broke the Needle*. In more recent times humorous fiction has been carried on by Geoff Dutton's well-known 'Doctor' stories, which first saw the light of day in the *SMC Journal*, and my own stories about Big Harry, Sorrowful Jones and the other disreputable characters who appear in my *Me and the Lads* series. But even these latter are based on some true incident, and I daresay Geoff Dutton's are too.

It stands to reason then that book-length mountain fiction of the humorous sort is pretty rare. Only two come to mind: Molly Lefebure's imaginative tale about a feline expedition to Scafell called *Scratch & Co.*, and W. E. Bowman's classic, *The Ascent of Rum Doodle*. Both parody the big Himalayan expedition, and though they both tail off a bit towards the end, they are glorious send-ups. *Rum Doodle* also utilizes some nineteenth-century pictures to illustrate the text in a way which is both clever and funny. It is said that we have to thank *Rum Doodle* for putting an end to all those appalling expedition books which tried to cash in on the success of Hunt's 1953 Everest volume. Well, maybe – certainly it is hard to take any expedition book seriously after reading *Rum Doodle*!

Examples of all the various kinds of mountain humour will be found in the following pages, either as complete articles or in extracts from longer pieces. They show the game in its many forms, and to keep up that theme I have divided them into three sections: *Playing at Home*, which is concerned with British climbing; *Playing Away*, which concerns overseas adventures; and *Offside*, which is more about people and things than places.

I. Playing at Home

Graham Sutton | The Man Who Broke the Needle

It was no place to have teeth out – an October morning in Borrowdale, with the clouds high, and only three more days of leave, and Ronnie dumping sacks and rope into the Doctor's old car, to go climbing on Gable.

But I'd no choice. An army marches on its belly, and I'd been marching on that rotten molar all yesterday; and the Doc swore he couldn't deaden it, it would really have to come out. So last night I'd made a date with the Keswick dentist – nice and earlyish, ten a.m. – and the Doc told him on the phone just what was wrong with me; and we both rubbed it into him that he could do his worst in the morning, but that he'd got to have me fit to go and climb again by midday; because it wasn't having the thing out I was grousing at (who wants an aching molar, anyhow?) but the waste of good time. So after breakfast, when we'd fixed a rendezvous, they made for Seathwaite and I caught the bus into town.

The dentist was there, all set: with his accomplice (I mean his anaesthetist) and with that sort of beastly cheerfulness they're so good at. I'd ordered gas, because I'd heard that you recover quicker from that, and I'd no wish to lose more time than I had to. But when he'd violated the tooth a bit, the chap said: 'H'm, trouble! I'd recommend an injection.'

I asked why. Somehow I never feel you can trust dentists.

He said: 'Gas may not give me time enough –' And then he added some intimidating prophecies about roots. But I stood firm. I said: 'Look here: I'm going to climb this afternoon if you pull my head off. And I can't climb full of dope. Gas goes off sooner, doesn't it?'

He dodged that; and countered me below the belt with another prophecy. 'If you come round before I'm through it won't be much fun –' This sounded rather geometrical to me; but I said I wasn't there for fun, and I'd chance it. I caught the two of them exchanging a nasty look; and I could see they weren't sure whether to humour me, or tell me to mind my own business. The accomplice picked up the dentist's needle-gun, and started practising an approach-shot; he lacked the delicacy of the dentist, who had put his pliers in a little shaving-jug and was pretending they weren't there. But I said: 'Gas or nothing!' And climbed on board.

So the accomplice laid aside the gun, on a swing-table in front of me, and began juggling with that sinister conglomeration of snakes that they pump gas in you with (*Death of Laocoon*, you know). And the dentist said open please, and rammed a gag in me: a thing that tasted like a cold hotwater-bottle, and felt like a dumbbell. He remarked heartily: 'You're a big fellow, aren't you! I'd hate *you* to get violent. What's your weight?'

And I said eighteen stone – at least I said hay-hee-ho, because of the gag. But of course he was only making talk; it didn't matter whether he could understand me or not. He went on, chattily:

'This gag is in case you bite! It wouldn't do to have you clench your teeth when I was giving you an injection; you might break the needle!'

I exclaimed: 'Huh-hi-hoch-hachiha –' Then I spat out the gag, and started again. 'But I'm not *having* an injection –'

He said: 'No, no. I don't suppose you are. But I can't operate with your mouth shut.' So he replaced the gag and asked if it was comfortable: sarcastically, I suspect. And I said: 'Hoch!' And the snake-charmer weighed in with his gas machine, and told me to inspire deeply. And I inspired, and hoped like billyo they'd have the *nous* not to begin too soon . . . And they didn't. And that was that.

After all, it was not too bad; I mean you don't actually feel the pangs of goodbye. I lay recovering in an ante-room, and read the obituaries in last week's *Cumberland News*, and sucked the hole with my tongue. I'd come in climbing-kit; and the first minute I felt good enough, I tottered out into the Keswick market-place and caught the Seatoller bus.

The Styhead track on a fine fresh October day would put anyone on his feet. When I arrived below the Napes the others weren't visible, but I heard their voices above. So I lay out on the high terrace under Eagle's Nest that climbers call the Dress Circle, and filled a pipe, and found it didn't go too well with my jaw, so I shoved it away, and began excavating in the hole again – it's queer, your tongue won't let ill alone with a place like that – and stared down at Wasdale. I'd done that many a score of times, but it's not a view you get tired of: a lovely jigsaw-tangle of bright little green fields, all shapes and sizes, like a chess-board gone mad; and the lake slaty-black; and the sea hanging high up in the air, twelve miles off.

But the main interest for this afternoon – what the dentist had left of it – was the ridges. There's as pleasant climbing here-abouts, you know, as anywhere on this earth: Napes Needle, for instance. You'll have seen photos of the Needle, of course. A rum-looking affair. It's been compared with lots of things; but what it most reminded *me* of, just then, was a great tusk of a molar. It sticks up out of the cliff's jaw, facing the Dress Circle: a big sharp pyramid, but steeper than Pharaoh's lot: the left wall pretty nearly vertical (I don't think it *can* be climbed: not by me anyhow), the right edge ragged against the sky, and the face all cracked into blocks. In the old days it used to be done by the central crack; and that's still the merriest way down – you just slide: as down banisters. But the ascent is less popular; the footholds were always thin; and they've been worn so smooth, and you're so liable to jam your leg and have to leave your boot behind, or perhaps even your breeches, that a lot of modest men rather jib at it and prefer to go upstairs by the ridge.

Just now the other two came down off Eagle's Nest, and we had some sandwiches (at least they had, my jaw wasn't too good) and then we all tumbled into Needle Gully and began to scramble up to our rock. It seemed the very thing for today: appropriate, and a nice heartening job of work, and not too long if I tired. The Doctor led it, by the ridge; and I came second on the rope; and Ron brought up the rear.

No end of a good climb it is, with teeth or without them. From the main crack you edge out horizontally, on rather sketchy holds with a long drop beneath; but once you're there, you'd be surprised how much less difficult it is than it looked. Nice, jagged, help-yourself-and-welcome stuff, with a belaying-pin the size of a cricket bat half-way up: and at the top a regular armchair of an anchorage, where you can brace your feet across a gap and safeguard the next man. Then comes a scramble up some easy rock to the shoulder; and there trouble begins.

You're on a platform: lots of room for three of you. And your next problem is to get up a smooth little wall, on which the top-storey stands. It's like a mantelshelf – they call it the Mantelshelf – a long ledge, chin-high, and four inches deep. You can catch hold of it, and then press-up on it, to put your knees where your hands are; and the whole job would be as easy as falling off a log – I mean as easy as not falling off a log – if only you had more room. Try climbing any ordinary mantelshelf and you'll see. You want to lean well forward across the shelf, but the top-wall won't let you. You must perform the trick erect, like a toy monkey; only the monkey's nailed on to the stick, and you're not. At home, you could catch hold of something like a picture-rail; but here there's nothing at all.

My turn came when the Doctor was perched on top, out of sight. And I just couldn't make it. Three times I pressed-up on the shelf; but when I tried to squirm a good knee on to it, I conked out and slid back. Ron mocked at me, from the platform: 'What's your weight, G.S.?'

I said: 'The dentist asked me that. I'm hay-hee-ho, less a few ounces for the tooth.'

Ron's voice came up: 'You've spoilt your balance, having that tooth out, it's left you too light in front and too heavy behind.'

I said: 'Forceps to you –!'

But in the end, by gosh, I got up. Half up, anyhow. I'd still the worst bit; I had to raise myself from my knees to my feet, without falling backwards.

It's not easy any time; and today, thanks to that beastly dentist probably, it defied me. So I did something very wrong: reached up and helped myself in secret to a nice pull on the rope. Most unorthodox. The wrongness is, that if you pull-up on a rope the leader feels that it's taut, and doesn't haul in the slack. So, as you rise, you get a two-or-three-foot loop hanging down by you; and if you come unstuck just then, of course you're going to drop so much clear. And that's what happened to *me*. I was just upright when my toe slipped, my knuckles grazed the rock, a

'As we lay there half dazed, and sorting ourselves, we heard a kind of a rumbling.'

stinging pain made me let go the rope and I swayed over backwards. I dropped two feet before the slack ran out, and my full hay-hee-ho came on the Doctor's rope with a bang.

I must explain now how the Doctor was fixed. He was up out of sight of us, on the flat summit of the final pyramid which measures six feet by three: with the rope belayed round his shoulder . . . People ask sometimes if it isn't worrying, on a rock-climb, to have nothing beneath you. Well, it's not, really; you don't think of it; and you couldn't do anything if you did. Much worse to have nothing above; the leader's job is to tie on to something firm above, in case the next man comes off, some flake, or spike. But on the Needle, you're on top of everything and there's nothing left to tie on to. Your only safeguard is to drape several loops of rope round the peak itself, beneath where you're sitting; you have to loop yourself below yourself – because there *is* no above. The Doctor had done that. But when I fell, the jerk on my rope dragged him off his perch and he half dropped, half slithered down the face of the pyramid, till his own belay held.

The whole thing happened in a breath; but you see how it landed us? I'd been left dangling over Ron, a few feet above the platform; the Doctor's fall released my rope and I came tumbling on to Ron, who collapsed with me. The Doctor's case was more serious. He must have come down a good twelve feet before the belay stopped him. Then the rope snapped; it wasn't built for such a strain; they make them good for a hundred-and-some-thing pounds dropping umpteen feet, probably in a vacuum; but the Doc's gravity is a bit plus-ish . . . Still, it broke his fall. The wonder was, it didn't bisect the beggar. It stopped him dead, a yard above the pair of us; and when it parted, down he slumped on to us.

But we weren't finished yet! As we lay there half dazed, and sorting ourselves, we heard a kind of a rumbling. And Ron let out one yell. And I looked up, and saw that the huge pyramid of the Needle-tip was adrift!

It's a poised block, you know: not part of the main structure. I had always heard you could vibrate the thing if you rocked on it. And now the mighty jerk we'd given it must have started it off. Not towards us, luckily; the fissure slopes towards the gully, and the block was creeping that way. It slunk down, almost imperceptibly at first, but soon faster: with a queer, frightful, grinding noise. And then it passed beyond its centre of gravity; and the noise stopped; and the whole thing leaned very gently outward, and fell.

It struck once, just above the crack. Then a long silence: minutes, it seemed like. And then a most almighty crash below, as it hit the bed of the gully. We craned after it; we thought we'd see it go on walloping down into Wasdale. But it never budged, just stuck embedded bottom-up in the loose scree of the gully. And a big mushroom-cloud of sunny dust spread on the air. And Ron and I hung, gaping down at it, and heard our own hearts beating.

The Doctor was still laid out; his fall had winded him. By and by, when he sat up, he got the devil of a shock to see the Needle-tip wasn't with us; he thought he must be delirious (doctors are easily alarmed about themselves: I daresay you've noticed that), but we assured him it was all correct, and he cheered up a little. And when he'd satisfied himself that he'd not smashed any ribs, we got down as quick as we could.

We didn't say much; we were too scared; and if we'd overturned the Albert Memorial we couldn't have felt more guilty. You see, the Needle is a sort of National Monument; men come back happily to do it again, year after year, from the far ends of the earth; and now . . .! So we just slid the crack, and dropped into the gully bed, and ploughed across with our eyes turned from the great foreign-body sticking there, and scrambled up to the Dress Circle again; and there we sat and took stock.

The Needle looked pretty awful without its tip. It looked forlorn and stumpy and undignified. It looked *wrong*. We stared at it without speaking; and – you know how it is, when you've come through a nasty fright and the reaction sets in, it plays queer tricks on you – Ron began to laugh.

He said: 'O Lord, G.S., you've been and done it now! You'll go down to history. The hiking heavyweight! The man who left no stone unturned! The man who crashed the old Needle! My hat, whatever will the Fell and Rock Club say? Oh, G.S., you've surpassed yourself –!'

I couldn't see anything to laugh about. I was too ashamed: like that chap in the *Ancient Mariner* – 'For I had done a hellish thing' – you know the passage I mean. And there's a tag in Scripture: 'Cursed is he that removeth his neighbour's landmark, amen!'

I said: 'Oh, shut up . . . I've two more days' holiday; but I'm off home tonight before this gets out.'

Ron rolled back, helpless. 'Gets out! Hear that, Doctor? How long d'you think we'll keep it dark? O Lord, I'm going to be sick –'

Then we heard nailed boots on the rocks, and three fellows hove in view. They'd been on Arrowhead, round the corner. And when the first man came in sight of where the Needle ought to be, he stopped dead. 'Great Scot! I say, George, look here –!'

Ron punched me: 'You're too late, G.S. – it's out!' And then he must needs jump up and point at me and say: 'He's broken the Needle!'

And the newcomers glared, and shook their fists at me, and said: 'The big stiff! He ought to be handcuffed!'

And Ron kept gurgling: 'It's out!'

I hadn't heart enough to say anything. I sat there overwhelmed with shame, with my eyes shut: feeble and limp. And the voices kept on at me: 'It's out . . . he's broken the Needle . . . ought to be handcuffed, the big stiff . . . it's OUT!'

At last I opened my eyes: and saw the accomplice groping on the floor, where I'd kicked all his bag of tricks: and beside me the dentist, holding up triumphantly a great pyramid of a tooth.

from *Fell Days* (1948)

G. D. Abraham | No Room at the Inn

The following amusing story is told of the times before the inn was enlarged. The parson in those days was a weird character, and one Easter Thursday, when occupying his usual chair in the bar-parlour, or rather kitchen, he was present when a party of Oxford dons invaded the place, demanding rooms when all available space was occupied. The jovial *curé*, in knee-breeches and clogs, took compassion on them and asked them to share his hospitality at the vicarage. His visitors perforce missed the following Sunday's climbing; the sermon which edified them instead was from the text, 'I was a stranger and ye took me in.' To the guests this seemed very appropriate, but they did not realize its full meaning until the day of reckoning was due. This came next morning when, as one of them aptly expressed it, they were presented with a bill twice as stiff as the Gable Needle; which of course was paid without a grumble.

※ from *British Mountain Climbs* (1909)

Samuel Turner | Ilam Rock

My next amusing episode occurred when I climbed the Watch Tower, or Ilam Rock, Dovedale, Derbyshire. My friend Holmes was not the famous Sherlock Holmes, but he was a genius in detecting the way through holes and caves all through Derbyshire; and after his climb of Monte Rosa he detected a climb which he thought I alone was the man to unravel. I journeyed to Alsop-in-the-Dale Station, near Buxton, Derbyshire, and by his assistance and that of the Rev. A. Wallaker of Buxton, we managed to get a rope over, but could not make it secure enough on the other side to be any use.

After this I climbed a little way up the rock, and it encouraged me, by letting a lump of limestone (of which it is composed) drop on my head, raising a big lump.

I came down, feeling rather seedy, and we adjourned to the hut at the foot of this rock to take what lunch the old man caretaker could give us. Dovedale is a pleasure place, and it was Bank Holiday, with plenty of trippers about, so while we were having lunch the old gentleman commenced to talk about this most attractive piece of rock, the Ilam Rock.

He said: 'That rock is over 200 feet high, from the River Dove at its foot. It has no place for anybody to get hold of to climb it, and it is quite vertical and overhanging in some places. There have been hundreds of parties trying to climb it, but they have never succeeded, and never will. The top of that rock is the place where the birds of Dovedale fly when they want to die, and it is covered by the skeletons of birds.' He continued: 'There are some men trying to climb it again today, but they will hurt themselves, like many more before them.' My companions interrupted the old gentleman by roaring with laughter, when I placed my hand on the big lump on my head.

We adjourned from lunch and I went at the climb with more determination than ever. I had previously not known it was such a difficult problem, or that many people had attempted it; but now I was sure, and Holmes also told me of some Alpine Club men who had given it up as impossible.

After carefully climbing the rock by the slowest and safest way possible, I got myself wedged into an overhanging chimney, the climax to the climb. As luck would have it, I was the exact fit to wedge myself into this crack, but it was such an awkward crack that it required all the strength I could exert to keep myself wedged tightly in and wriggle up in snail-like movements. The crack was only forty feet long, but it took me about an hour to get to the top; then I almost slipped off the rock as I crawled out at the top. I was absolutely winded as I sat on the top of the lowest side of the rock.

The crowd down below gave me a great cheer, but the old man was in the crowd, and did not agree that his famous rock was climbed until I got to the other end, which was higher. The rock was about two feet wide at the very top, then it suddenly slanted out to about eight feet thick, and the middle to the base of the rock was about twelve to twenty feet thick. It was blowing very hard, but I would not crawl on hands and knees, and it required very careful walking to get to the other end. When I did reach there I found it was overhanging. I stood up on the edge, and the trippers who had cameras took photographs of me and again cheered. This was the only time I climbed to the applause of the crowd. Carefully turning round I walked back over bones of birds and hawks as the old man had said, and after leaving a penny on the top under a stone and my name on some paper for the next climber, I began the descent. By this time a Sunday-school choir-party were singing hymns at the base underneath the overhanging crack. As I climbed down the crack I found it all I could do to prevent myself tumbling out. If I had done so, I don't think I would have killed myself, but the chap singing 'Abide with me' below would have had a shock.

I consider the Ilam Rock climb more difficult than any Cumberland climb.

This climb was gazetted in all the papers in the north of England. It is a well-known piece of rock, and of the most extraordinary formation, so that it is known all over Derbyshire. That climb was six years ago, but nobody has made a second climb, although there have been numerous attempts by well-equipped parties. Two of my friends were in that district last year, and paid a visit to this rock, and asked the old hut-keeper if anyone had ever climbed the Ilam Rock. He said: 'Nobody except Sam Turner has ever climbed to the top of yond rock.'

❋ from *My Climbing Adventures in Four Continents* (1911)

| # Chalking
It Up

'Come along now, gentlemen, PLEASE,' repeated Daddy McKay almost testily, shepherding glasses on to his impatient tray and flicking his napkin through our animated discussion. But we were slow to leave the back bar that night and the Doctor was still defiant as he struggled into his raincoat at the door, Daddy McKay determinedly freeing a sleeve. 'It's the old days again; the end of your artificial aids.'

He had been lent some Hard Men's Glossies, and his imagination billowed chalk dust and waves of golden Apollos swarming effortlessly up the impossible, ropeless and shirtless (it was the Fawcett era). Climbing was free again, chalk was scarcely an Aid, no more than boots, and quite invisible if tinted to match the rock ('Torridonian would need, let me see, BS04D43: say, Manders' *Copper Rose* or something like that . . .'). But Scottish orogeny is diverse and contorted, and it seemed a whole palette might be required to satisfy the hues encountered on a single route. The Apprentice, veteran of countless gritted hours with fellow Weasels on rain-battered rugosities, dissolved these calciferous enthusiasms as best he could; he preferred a rope. I, as so often on the hill, followed his lead; for the prospect of trails of polychromatic guano – however tastefully selected – lengthening with the weather down our favourite buttresses was not attractive. Also, although we appreciated the Doctor's company, and his transport, for frequent escalades of the earlier Scottish classics, we were doubtful of his ability, powdered or plain, to adhere sufficiently to much above Severe (Winter was a different matter). His easy denunciations stung us. So, unwisely, before we parted at the Mound the Apprentice invited him to join us that weekend at the Ben, on a new HVS – just to see what it was like. And equally unwisely, the Doctor had agreed.

'Ha, *Constipation*, is it? Yes, I've heard of that. Pretty stiff, by all accounts. But an experience. Even if a limited one: you chaps –' We choked off another tirade, and pushed him homeward. 'Now mind you mug up your ropework. And no bloody chalk . . .' was the Apprentice's parting shot. The vision of the Doctor leaping heroically ahead, in dust and bathing trunks, up two hundred leering metres of vertical Lochaber was, that night, most amusing.

It grew less amusing as the weekend approached, and we were strangely silent during the Saturday journey north. The Doctor's old Mercedes lumbered more thoughtfully round the bends in Glencoe, its usual elephantine squeals reined in. After lunch on the shore beyond Ballachulish the Apprentice whistled tunelessly, I plucked grassheads, and the Doctor poked about among seaweed on the boulders. None of us mentioned The Climb, not even by evening when we reached the hut.

We were greeted by the occupants, sundry youths of lurid and basic communicatory skills hailing from the more abrasively north of England. They had, it appeared, gained unlawful entry several days before, and generously offered us the three remaining bunks. Their leader was one Sodder, a formidable XS exponent of whose exploits on alcohol and crag the Apprentice and – since his magazine excursions – the Doctor were well informed. As a large, legitimate and uncompromisingly Glaswegian party was also booked for the hut that night, and was at this instant celebrating thirstily its arrival at the Fort, we gloomily predicted a disturbed prelude to tomorrow's epic.

In the hour or so before the engagement we heard the Englishmen had suffered no trouble from *Constipation* and had, superfluously enough, gone on to take in an adjacent shocking artificial, *Purgative*, dismantling that of aid except half-way up the crux – a quite holdless bulging slab over a horrible, truly aperient, exposure. They had removed even that peg afterwards, for the benefit of their successors . . . It would be at least an XS, climbed free.

The Doctor, scenting chalk, engaged them in earnest conversation. Unfortunately, his incautious extempores in magazine lingo gave them the startled impression that he intended to climb *Constipation* without a rope. The crimson Apprentice was about to cross to the guffaws and explain, when the doorway was filled with Glaswegians; then silence; then expletives.

We managed a few hours' sleep after the battle, one of Bannockburnian intensity and conclusion; and then padded painfully to the foot of our climb. We wore E.B.s, the Doctor his old gym shoes, bared to the canvas ('probably illegal' . . .) and were laden with ironmongery of all configurations and clatter – clusters and particles of wires, hexcentrics, bongs, étriers . . . and ropes, ropes, ropes. The Apprentice was taking no chances. He kept instructing the Doctor on the red rope, the green rope, the fixed rope, the free rope, this rope and that rope. The Doctor nodded sagely, obviously and irritatingly wishing to understand little of it. As he strode, his coils opened and shut, disclosing a small canvas bag tied to his waistband. Chalk . . .? Chalk, it must be. If the English saw us . . . From the disgruntled tents of the vanquished far up the Allt a'Mhùillin (whence they could, at their own convenience, pollute the hut's alleged water supply) we imagined the first faint jeers. But we said nothing.

The initial pitches were fairly uneventful: steep dry rock in early sun. The Apprentice had struck form. I followed adequately despite my burden of prophylaxis, and the Doctor rattled up behind, multijointedly competent as a harvestman crossing a flysheet. But he was troubled by the prolixity of ropes. I gathered them up before him, as one conjures the cords of a disobedient Venetian blind. He arrived and cast further superfluity at my feet. 'Most tiresome, all these unnecessary ropes. No wonder they hardly use them nowadays.' He held out his arms like one accepting wool; I wound him about suitably and turned upwards again.

There were of course minor anxieties. As when the Doctor suddenly stuck. In mid-swarm. He was surmounting a roof, a narrowing crack on his left. He strained and swore. No use.

'I think I'm stuck.' Then, more specifically, 'These damned things are caught somewhere below.' Further information revealed that he could not spare a single limb, and his neck (surprisingly) was not long enough to allow his teeth full play. Praying and cursing, I secured his ropes and abseiled down. The nuts on the wire slings attached to his harness had travelled beside him up the crack; when it narrowed they had fulfilled the intentions of their designer. Extrication proved lengthy. I relieved him of slings. A similar incident occurred shortly afterwards on an outward-pressing wall, to the anguish of our leader, spread on a balance stance out of sight above; it involved a mysterious loop of rope about the Doctor's rucksack and a mutual tying and re-tying in a parabiotic embrace on a half-hearted wrinkle of rock, and was complicated by a hook in his fishing hat refusing to leave my ear. Clearly he was not to be trusted with this mileage of rope. We were already garlanded grotesquely; soon he would be a cocoon. I pruned him of rucksack, ironmongery and spare coils and left him with a suitably modest bell-pulling repertoire, the bare minimum of attachment.

It is the next pitch, the pendulum pitch, that still shakes our memories. *Constipation* entails only a brief pendulum – as its name implies, it concentrates on a fairly rigid line – but the Doctor, drunk from his liberation, leapt lankily rightward from so far left he outshot the route, collided with a brutal rib on the other side, twisted, and vanished out of sight behind it. He did not come back. I pulled the red rope. No reply. The green one. It pulled back. His seventy-five inches were presumably still consecutive.

Their retrieval was less obvious. The rib cut off sight and coherent sound. Only a muffle. I roared instructions. Only a muffle. Then, a high whoop of derision. It was the English. Even farther to our right, in several parties, on fearsome lines. And much enjoying our plight. The ribaldries of Sodder were particularly displeasing to the Apprentice, who was informed from that embarrassing source of the fate of our colleague.

'Yer know were e is? E's on *Purgative*. An e's there for keeps. Right under the bloody crux!'

We froze. His return demanded a computery of rope-twiddling impossible to convey through twenty metres of indifferent andesite. And clearly the English were going to enjoy the situation as long as possible. Last night would not soon be forgotten. They began to sing 'Will yer no come baaack again . . .'

Pushing rightward on vanishing balance holds the Apprentice managed to look over an impassable gulf to our companion. He shouted down instructions to both of us. No easy task, with the Auld Enemy jamming the wavelength ('*Bonnie Chaarlie's noo awaaah . . .*'). The inevitable had to happen. The Doctor, none too clear anyway about which of the unidentifiable ropes to clip

'He looked up, saw us, grinned, and waved perilously.'

or unclip or haul in or let out, and counterinstructed by the echoes booming about his vertical darknesses, let slip the only line that could have ensured his return to us – that even joined us . . . The end snaked down into limbo. We heard a muffled 'Blast!'

The English, if they were sympathetic, did not show it. The singing stopped.

'E's chucked off is bloody rope like e said e would. E's goin to do *Purgative* free! Ah, yer can't 'old im back, can yer? Good ole Golden Boy!' Unfeeling roars of laughter. Whistles, hoots; then *'Scotland the Brave'*, much off-key.

Although we knew the Doctor's remarkable powers of survival, we began to sweat. I struggled up slabs and roofs to the Apprentice, and crabbed out to the edge overlooking *Purgative*. The Doctor occupied its one gesture at a ledge, but seemed in good form, hat rammed firmly on, the usual sign of determination. We could not cross down to him; but would have to descend *Constipation*, peg up *Purgative*, work out runners and then somehow gather him in. A long job. He could not abseil from his present position; to climb down was unthinkable; to climb up would bring him almost alongside us, but was equally unthinkable – the crux of *Purgative* free and without protection! And now a thin mist moistened the rocks . . . It might have to be helicopters, or Pitfoulie. O, the shame of it . . . Comment and songs continued ('Come on, Jock, straight up, that's it' . . . 'Yer 'alf-way there already, mate' . . . '*You take the 'igh road and I'll* . . .').

The Apprentice whipped his ropes and hammered in the first abseil peg. I gazed fascinated at the Doctor.

'Lord, what's he doing now?' The Apprentice paused; and stared, too. The singing stopped. Whistles died.

He had hauled his loose end back, tied it in a loop and, after a couple of shots, miraculously lassoed an evil razor-edged spike to his right. A parapsychological belay, indeed. He looked up, saw us, grinned, and waved perilously. And then, balancing outward against all his years of Alpine anecdote, put his left hand surreptitiously into his little canvas bag.

'Chalk! He's not going to try the crux on CHALK?!!'

His hand emerged, pressed the rock in front of him firmly, patted it, and returned to the bag. Then he patted the rock a little higher up, similarly.

Chalk? The English were as dead silent as us. Sodder was poised on one toe and a finger, agape. Chalk?

A few more gropings in the bag and pattings, and he began to move up the appalling bare bulge of slab that gave *Purgative* its name. Not true. Our mouths cracked with drought.

He groped again. More pattings. And up another metre or so. The crux is not so much vertical as impossibly smooth and holdless. Yet he climbed the six metres of it as deliberately as if he were moving from invisible pimple to pimple, or pick-scratch to pick-scratch as in his tales of the moonlit Brenva; even the venomously gentle detachment of belay from spike did not disturb him. One slip . . .

Incredibly, falling was far from our thoughts. We were hypnotized by his proceeding up that unthinkable slab. Of course, he had a Glenmorangie reach, but . . .

He was suddenly just below us on the right. He had climbed the crux. He gripped, white-knuckled and thankfully enough, its final rim. He grinned. A deep breath, and he mantelshelfed on to a stance, stood up, stretched, and rubbed his arms.

'Can you chuck me a rope? Might as well use one now. The rest's a doddle, but the easy bits are always the most dangerous ... And all your tomfoolery took it out of me at the beginning.'

Our emotion was great as we lassoed his outstretched arm, and became greater with the applause from across the cliff, punctuated by only a few face-saving catcalls. The English are sportsmen yet.

The respectful spell was somewhat broken by a subsequent barrage of queries. They possessed the same tenor:

"Ow the —— did a daft ole — like that get up *Purgative*?'

How indeed? When we finally all arrived at the top of *Constipation*, which gave us little trouble after our remedial dose of its neighbour, the Apprentice and I, still trembling, put the question in less generally philosophical terms.

'What the devil have you got in that bag? Plaster of Paris?'

He smiled avuncularly, and untied the canvas. He held it high and shook it upside down over the Apprentice's doubtful palm. Two or three moist conical objects dropped out.

The Apprentice drew his hand away hurriedly. The objects fell to the scree. The Doctor bent and picked them up.

'Lucky I had enough. I was just running out.'

'What *are* they, for heaven's sake?' We stared uncomprehendingly. The answer was simple. He held it out.

'Limpets. *Patella vulgata*. Got them yesterday on the shore. Not the rockpool sort, but the real knobbly high-water-mark jobs. Tough; used to exposure. Can stand waves of 25 tons to the square yard. Thought they might come in handy. Winthrop Young recommended 'em. Of course you put your weight on 'em gradually. Give 'em time to suck. Too quick dislodges 'em. Interesting technique.

Not really artificial: sort of Combined Tactics – after all, they *are* alive ...'

We were still speechless.

'Ha, you thought they were chalk? So they are – chalk on the hoof. It's lucky the rock got damp just then and kept 'em happy, though I did bring some sea water, just in case.'

We rattled down the path. Neither the Apprentice nor I, still shaking, could face Tower Ridge, and the Doctor was not keen to descend *Purgative*. 'You know, they're chancy beasts.'

That evening Sodder came down, to see the Doctor. They had a long discussion, as between equals. Sodder went away after only half a bottle of Strath Hashie; he appeared preoccupied.

'He's going to try *Purgative* solo tomorrow.' We asked about the limpets. 'I mentioned them in passing. I don't think he took it in. You technicians are terribly limited. And it'll rain tonight. He'll never see them. They'll have moved, or been eaten, by the morning. You know, you need a fresh lot, each time.'

from *Climber and Rambler* (1982)

Claude E.
Benson

The Trippercrock

(A very *Loose* Carol
of the Lake District)

'Twas dammot! and the flicksy sails
    Did fly and flimmer o'er the wave;
All toorisd were the Borrodails,
    And the Beercasks outgave.

Beware the Trippercrock, my son,
    The glass that flies, the stones that crash;
Beware the Pop-Pop bird, and shun
    The frumious Bottlesmash.

He bound his clinknale sole on foot;
    Longtime the lantic foe he sought;
Then rested well by the Pinnakell,
    And groused awhile in thought.

And as in thought he humpied there,
    The Trippercrock, with lingo blue,
Hurled piffling through the scorfle air
    And hurtled as it threw.

One-two! Click-click! and sharp and quick
    The clinknale foot went clitter-clack;
Till, when it swore to chuck no more,
    He went jodumphling back.

And hast thou smit the Trippercrock?
    Come to my arms, my plucksome boy!
A safious time, Kerloo, Kerlimb!
    He kaykwalked in his joy.

'Twas dammot! and the flicksy sails
    Did fly and flimmer o'er the wave;
All toorisd were the Borrodails,
    And the Beercasks outgave.

✳ from *Fell and Rock Journal*

Walt Unsworth | Gone to Earth

I do not think you could call the lads real animal lovers. It's not that they actually hated animals, but just that they never thought about them, or if they did then it was with a cold detachment quite alien to our national character.

This antipathy extended even to dogs. I doubt if any of the lads ever owned a dog, and if they did then the poor bloody mongrel would have had no doggy vitamins to slaver over, but would have had to make do with common steak like the rest of us. The image of Big Harry, for example, squatting on his massive haunches and murmuring 'Poochy, poochy, poochy' to one of those little miniatures is not one which springs readily to mind, you must admit. He once kicked a bulldog up the arse, mark you, but that was because the savage brute bit him for trespassing, so it should not be construed as a sign of affection.

I am fully aware that this sort of attitude puts the lads beyond the pale for many people. I mean all those animal lovers who spend hours grooming their horses so that they can hunt foxes, or pat their dog with real affection as they wait to empty both barrels into some unsuspecting grouse. And yet, despite this, the lads had a compassion which went deeper than one would imagine, looking at their craggy, weather-beaten faces.

It puts me in mind of the time Sorrowful Jones took part in a fox hunt: not officially, of course, because Sorrowful was not really one of the county set.

It happened one spring in the Lake District, when Sorrowful was out of work and spending a few idle days alone, wandering the fells and sleeping rough. He had started his walk in Langdale as usual; had a flaming row with a couple of blokes at the Wall End Barn, and escaped into a westering sun over Rossett Ghyll to Wasdale, there to commune with nature.

He made his bed by some big boulders below the awful scree

slopes which sweep down from Scafell Crag: a cliff of sheer, black, forbidding rock and not the sort of place I would choose to sleep, myself. But Sorrowful is funny that way, something of a masochist. He's the only bloke I know who *prefers* to sleep on hard rock. I reckon he has a Japanese ancestor somewhere in his twisted family tree – although the permanent yellow cast to his skin comes from not washing too often.

He slept until the warm spring sun was into the sky, then he rose and stretched, batted the dust out of his clothes, and scrambled over to a nearby beck where he obtained a panful of water for the coffee which formed his breakfast. He had two sweet cups that morning, bulked out by a forgotten crispbread which he discovered in his rucksack, then he packed away his petrol stove and mug and prepared for the forthcoming day.

And a lovely day it was too; such a day as can only happen in the Lakes in spring. The sunshine made the rocks glow with warmth, the becks tinkled like fairy pianos, and the new lambs bleated for their mothers in the valley below. The sky was blue, with puffs of pure white cloud to break the monotony, and even old Scafell itself seemed less broody, as though it acknowledged the day as perfect. What with all these signs of Nature's annual rebirth, and the warmth and promise of the day, Sorrowful felt pretty good. As he walked towards the cliffs he even burst into snatches of song:

> Caviare comes from the virgin sturgeon,
> The virgin sturgeon is a very fine fish,
> The virgin sturgeon needs no urgin',
> That's why caviare is my dish.

He was trying to remember the second verse of this immortal ballad, which had something to do with grandpa chasing grandma up a tree, when he came face to face with a fox.

Now there are a great many foxes in the Lake District but this was the first time that Sorrowful had ever seen one so close, and it is difficult to imagine which was the more surprised of the two. On balance, I reckon the fox – seeing as how there are lots of foxes but only one Sorrowful Jones.

Whatever effect the appearance of Sorrowful had on the fox's mind we shall never know, for the animal was already in a state of terror. It made no move to escape; instead it just lay on the ledge where it had ensconced itself, panting away so that its shaggy golden coat heaved in and out like the bosom of a film starlet doing weight-lifting exercises.

Although Sorrowful was not much of a judge of horseflesh, he could tell the fox was a young one, that it had been running hard, and that it was all but buggered, as the saying goes.

'Poor little sod,' said Sorrowful, aloud to the fox. 'What you been up to, then? Been tryin' to get up the crag, 'ave yer?'

The fox just lay, panting, its eyes not leaving Sorrowful's grubby face for an instant.

'You don't seem 'urt,' Sorrowful mused on, 'but yer must 'ave been runnin' like 'ell to get in this state.'

Then, cutting through the soft spring air like a butcher's knife, he heard the excited yapping of hounds, and looking up he saw the tiny piebald bodies of fifteen or twenty dogs rounding the shoulder of the mountain and scrabbling like mad things up the steep scree, darting this way and that, looking for the scent, their long tails waving with pleasure. Some way behind the hounds came the huntsmen, stumbling and cursing among the boulders but intent to be in at the kill.

' 'Ello then,' exclaimed Sorrowful to the fox, grasping at once the essentials of the situation. 'You're in a right fix, ain't you, mate? A bloody great crag up your backside an' a howlin' mob out front. They're out to get you, mate, an' no mistake.'

The fox kept its brown eyes steadfastly on Sorrowful's as if appealing for help.

Now I must make it clear that in the normal way of things, Sorrowful Jones doesn't give a bugger about foxes. He is not anti-blood-sport and he thinks aniseed is the stuff you make sweets from, but right then, at that moment in time, he could no more have stood by and seen that fox slaughtered than if it had been a suckling babe in the path of advancing Dervishes.

He had a sudden inner revulsion at the idea that people should turn one of God's cathedrals, Scafell, into a sacrificial altar. Before the fox knew what was happening, Sorrowful scooped it up and with a deft movement thrust it down the front of his anorak. Then he turned and ran towards the mountain for sanctuary.

*

Scafell Crag does not show up well from a distance unless you happen to pick exactly the right vantage point, so that when you come up to it, it is something of a surprise, not to say shock. It is easily the biggest mass of rock in the Lakes: towering walls and aggressively thrusting buttresses seamed with steep, dank gullies. From the middle distance it looks formidable; from close by it looks impossible.

And yet, when you know the place and have done mortal combat with it, you know it can be beaten. There are ledges and ways between ledges, and Sorrowful Jones knew them well.

Clutching his fox to his breast, Sorrowful scrambled to the foot of the rocks.

At first he thought he would escape up the long shoot of loose scree known as Lord's Rake, but the idea of toiling up such a steep slope under a hot sun did not appeal to him one bit, and anyway, he quickly realized that the dogs could follow and even overtake him. Then he thought of Slingsby's Route, which is a climb generously supplied with holds, but he remembered that it involved a rather nasty chimney overhanging a big drop, and whilst there might be room in the chimney for himself he was not sure he could manage it carrying a fox.

So in the end he just hit the cliff slap on and began to climb. He was barely in time, too, for as he stepped on to the rock the first of the dogs snapped at his heels. Their frustration at being so blatantly robbed of their birthright was something awful to hear.

The going was easy and within a few minutes Sorrowful reached a broad, grassy ledge, where he paused to wipe the perspiration from his brow and to see how the fox was getting along. He opened his anorak zip and the creature popped out its head to grin wickedly at the howling dogs some twenty feet below. At this piece of impertinence they howled even louder.

'They're dead narked, Foxy, an' no mistake,' observed Sorrowful, giving his charge a pat on the head.

Now, it is common knowledge that a dog is an animal with a fair degree of nous, and these particular dogs, being born and bred in the mountains, did not intend being thwarted by a bit of steep rock. When they discovered that they could not make a direct frontal assault on the cliff they switched off the old scent gland and reverted to natural cunning. They scouted around to see whether they could reach Sorrowful (and his fox) by an outflanking movement.

The moment Sorrowful realized what the dogs were about he knew he was in trouble. The ledge upon which he rested sloped down to his right and came so close to the ground that any dog with a bit of spring in its legs could easily reach it. Quickly, he pushed the fox's snout back inside his jacket again and began to climb higher.

A dozen of the dogs had meanwhile found the key to the ledge and had jumped aboard like four-legged pirates. When they found that their prey had gone once again, their fury knew no bounds. They wasted no time in baying for the moon, but got to work sniffing their way around the problem.

It was positively uncanny the way those dogs could find ledges and flakes with which to ascend the cliff. Before long some of them were once again level with Sorrowful, and would have reached him had he not beaten a quick, upwards retreat.

Fortunately for Sorrowful, the climbing was easy, but the dogs managed to follow, somehow. No sooner had he reached a ledge than some dog would appear on the one below. They were literally chasing him up the cliff.

Of course, things couldn't go on like that for long. The climbing got progressively more difficult and the ledges smaller and less frequent. The dogs began to feel the strain. They became fewer: half a dozen, four, two, until at last there was only one big hound, a black bastard with a brown eye patch, which kept up the chase.

It seemed able to follow Sorrowful wherever he went, that dog. It scrambled up a chimney after him, and Sorrowful claims it even laybacked a crack, but that I find hard to believe. He insists, however, that it was a damn sight better climber than Piss-eyed Pete, which I am prepared to accept.

By the time the black hound called quits, they were a considerable way up the cliff and Sorrowful was dead scared. The holds had diminished to almost nothing and the ledges were negligible. He was lost on that gaunt crag, with only a fox for company.

Somehow, he managed to keep going; always choosing what seemed the easiest way, until eventually he came to a great amphitheatre in the rocks. He recognized it at once as the bowl which funnels down into Moss Ghyll and his confidence came storming back. This was home ground. Within half an hour he was standing on the rocky summit of the mountain.

He glanced around apprehensively just to make sure the black dog had not followed him, but the only thing to meet his senses was the distant barking of hounds, far, far below, mingled with an occasional huntsman's shout and the frantic parping of a horn.

The fox scurried off, the moment Sorrowful opened his anorak, without so much as a glance back at his rescuer.

'Ungrateful bastard,' murmured Sorrowful. 'I wonder if foxes 'ave fleas?' He scratched at the thought, but if the fox did have fleas it had taken them with it.

The din from below grew to outrageous proportions. At first Sorrowful pretended not to notice but after a while the caco-phonous sound jarred his nerves. It seemed as though the whole of Wasdale was a pit of howling canines.

With a heavy sigh, Sorrowful picked up his rucksack and made his way towards Broad Stand, the easy way down. The noise disturbed the peace of the hills, and made him restless, but more than that he had developed an intense curiosity. He wanted to see what was going on down below.

It took him far less time to descend the mountain than it had to climb it. There was just one short, nasty bit which demanded his attention and then he was able to slide down a groove which landed him on the narrow ridge dividing Scafell from the neighbouring Pike. From there it was only a matter of minutes before he was once again at the foot of the great crag.

Now, Sorrowful Jones is not the kind of bloke you can easily surprise. He has a poker face which he got through playing poker, and he has been around a lot. In his short but crowded life he has seen most things so that there is little left with which to surprise him. But when he reached the foot of Scafell Crag that day, he was amazed.

Above him towered the great black buttresses of the crag, soaring for hundreds of perpendicular feet into the blue sky. At its foot, a group of huntsmen were dancing a kind of jig, which at first sight Sorrowful took to be some sort of ritual – like you

see on those travel films from Nepal. When this flash of fantasy
had passed, however, he could see that the huntsmen were not
dancing at all. They were hopping with rage.

And they had just cause. Scattered all over the soaring face of
the cliff on ledges great and small was a multitude of dogs.

There were brown dogs on black ledges and black dogs on
brown ledges. There were sitting dogs, standing dogs and dogs
on the trot like caged lions. Above all there were howling dogs
– for every single hound in the pack was stuck fast.

Sorrowful ambled over the scree to the dancing huntsmen
and struck up a conversation with a fiery-countenanced old boy
who seemed to be in a position of authority.

'They're stuck, mate,' remarked Sorrowful, indicating the
dogs.

The Master of Foxhounds gave him a look which would have
withered a fully matured oak, but Sorrowful pretended not to
notice. 'How did it 'appen, then?' he asked, innocently.

'You look like a climber, young fella: can't you get 'em down?'

'The damned brutes must have followed the fox up the crag,' replied the huntsman. 'Extraordinary business, what? We were all too far behind to see it clearly, or stop 'em. Now they're stuck up there.' He looked at Sorrowful hopefully and added, 'You look like a climber, young fella: can't you get 'em down?'

A young pup, which had been too small to keep up with the rest of the pack, had been standing by its master's legs, when suddenly it smelt the scent of fox on Sorrowful's anorak. With an infant bound it sprang at him, yapping excitedly.

'Down, Brutus! Down, boy!' commanded the Master. 'Dammit! Don't you know the difference between Man and Fox, yet? Can't think what's got into the blasted creatures today!'

'I'm used to bein' hunted, so don't mind me,' said Sorrowful, catching the dog a clip on the earhole which immediately stopped its malarky. The pup looked hurt and puzzled: nobody had ever told him that if you came too close to a fox-smell it belted you like a steam hammer.

'What about the pack?' moaned the Master.

Sorrowful shook his head. 'I'm only a poor soddin' rambler, mate, so I can't help yer.'

He wandered away, leaving the huntsmen to solve their problem as best they might. Down the scree he went, then along a sylvan greensward until he came to the valley floor and the cluster of cottages and the whitewashed old inn from whose windows men first gazed at crags with eyes that saw truth and adventure. He bought a pint of ale and some bread and cheese and consumed his repast in the glowing warmth of the afternoon sun.

That night he found again his old shelter spot on the rough stones and he lay down, contented. In front of him Scafell rose blackly etched against the purple night sky: an ebony outline of serrated towers. Less than an hour before, with the aid of torches and miles of rope, the last of the dogs had been recovered from the crag and the caterwauling had died away as the huntsmen returned home. Now it was still and dark and as Nature intended.

Sorrowful belched loudly, turned over, and fell asleep.

❋ from *Climber and Rambler* (1978)

Kevin
Fitzgerald

'I'm a Sick Man, Fitzgerald'

A stroll with Alan Hargreaves

In the early spring of 1951, or it may have been 1952, my doctors thought I needed a rest. 'Go to a place where you can potter about on your own,' they said. 'But nothing strenuous, mind: take a book into the open air and sit down often if you go for a walk.' I knew just the place for all that and I sent a telegram to Mr Christopher Briggs. He met me at Colwyn Bay, smiled grimly at the hundred feet of alpine hemp Lorimer Richardson had asked me to carry up for him, and put me into a room labelled 'Tryfan'.

I was having a drink after dinner with Tony Moulam, at that time theoretically engaged in a one-man reading party for his degree, when there was a minor disturbance in the hall. 'That will be Alan,' Tony said. 'I don't think you've met him?'

I was introduced to Mr Hargreaves, who thought he could manage half a pint. 'I must be careful,' he said. 'My days for all that drinking and larking about are very much over. I'm a sick man, Fitzgerald.'

I took a close look at this famous character. I had heard him called 'The Little Man', and that was what we had called the chief cowpoke in our outfit in Western Canada in 1926/7. I remembered that our little man had dealt rather more than adequately one afternoon with fourteen and a half stone of angry Red Indian called Bulling George. I also remembered a night in Devonshire in 1921 when half a dozen six-footers like me had failed to control a young man who, when sober, rather liked his nickname of 'Tiny Mac'. Finally, as I looked at Mr Hargreaves I recalled a dreadful affair in a Derbyshire public house in 1930. The police reserves from Sheffield arrived too late to save the bar from my friend 'Little Jimmy' and it took eight of them to get him into their van.

It is clear then that I had met some other little men in my time, but one is never too old to refuse to learn. I could easily have run away but instead I talked happily with Mr Hargreaves as the night brought various unshaven persons in from the surrounding countryside. I observed that he knew them all. 'No,' he said to each individual greeting. 'I'm afraid not. I'm a pretty sick man; only here for twenty-four hours or so to get a breather. I simply must rest.' He said much the same thing while we were washing up about two in the morning. He had just demonstrated to an unbeliever that it was quite easy, given what he called 'some general sense of balance', to eat a cheese and onion sandwich while standing on one's head in the middle of a room. 'Damn silly, really,' he remarked as we said good-night. 'Shouldn't do that kind of thing when I'm as ill as this. May see you tomorrow if I feel better.'

About ten o'clock next day I was sitting outside on the little white bench and wondering if I could perhaps get as far as the causeway and back before dark when Mr Hargreaves stood before me. 'What about a stroll?' he asked. I told him that I was not well enough for more than the gentlest exercise and he laughed. 'Look at me,' he said, 'I don't think I could get a mile from this hotel if I tried. I'm not just off-colour like you, Fitzgerald, I'm a sick man. Get your boots on and let's see what we can do. I've asked young Moulam to come along; we need someone fit to take care of us.'

I got very wet crossing the river. It was full and the stones were a foot or so under water. 'You want to remember what I was saying last night about balance,' Hargreaves said as he and Tony pulled me out. 'It's never any use blundering about at random. Always leads to trouble sooner or later.'

I caught them up about an hour later. Moulam was on something he called a 'problem crack' and Hargreaves was about six feet up on a large boulder nearby. As I lay down he climbed with extreme care to the heather and joined me. He pointed with a piece of meat from his haversack at some long scratches in a slate outcrop at the foot of the boulder. 'See those,' he said. 'Some ignorant fool must have jumped off. I bet he hit the mountain twenty or thirty feet down after that.' I remembered a day with Hilton-Jones and his happy cry of 'Your first fall; are you all right?' 'Yes,' I said to Hargreaves. 'He was an ignorant fool, that's for sure.'

They were waiting for me and looking at a wild goat when I had found my way off that wet plateau at the top of the miner's track and had begun stumbling about on the screes at the other side. 'You make a lot of noise with your feet, Fitzgerald,' Hargreaves said, getting up as I sat down. 'I'm afraid we haven't time to hang about if we're to get to the top.'

'Top of what?' I asked. 'I shan't be able to go much further; I'm all in now.'

'Top of Tryfan,' Hargreaves said. 'It's no distance from here and a pity to come as far as this and do nothing.' He looked down at me as I lay at his feet. 'I don't believe you eat enough,' he said. He put his hand into his haversack and dredged out a bit of cold bacon. I can still see it. There were raisins adhering to it and it was smeared with chocolate. 'Have a bit of this,' he said.

It was as Dr Bridges aptly observed in his *Testament of Beauty*: 'Late in my long journey when I had clomb to where the path was narrowing and the company few.' Three feet above me stood Hargreaves and Moulam. I lay in a little trough of rock. 'Look,' Hargreaves said. 'That's the summit forty feet from here. You can ease out of there and walk up, you know you can.' He moved a foot to his left and stood looking down at something. 'Just get to where I am, Fitzgerald, and you can hang over the finest precipice in Wales.' I went on clinging to the sides of my trough.

About ten minutes later I heard boots on rock and two men, strangers to me, joined Moulam and Hargreaves. The committee of four stood at the head of my trough and considered my situation. One of the newcomers offered a solution. He smiled and waved. 'Don't think about anything,' he said. 'Make your mind a blank and flow up to me.' The proprieties had been outraged. 'I don't think you've met, have you?' Hargreaves said. 'Mr Geoffrey Sutton, Mr Kevin Fitzgerald.'

'How do you do,' I said.

Time passed and I made my proposition. 'If I move out of here and go to the top will you promise I can sit down? Will you promise that?'

Hargreaves seemed astonished. 'Good Lord, yes. As long as you like. Need a rest myself. Not at all fit.'

On the summit we looked for mice and put sardine tins out of sight. I declined an invitation to try the jump from Adam to Eve. I also declined to sit on top of either. I thought that in perhaps an hour I might be able to think about another move.

'Good thing you had that rest in that little trough,' Hargreaves said. 'We don't want to be up here in the dark.'

We started down, as the mountaineering books say, and that was something I could do in those days. The hope of perhaps crashing to unconsciousness lent wings to my feet, and I was still with the party when we arrived back at the path across the scree.

I saw them, every now and again, until we reached the top of the miners' track. It was dark then and cold. I had not been able to breathe properly for some time. They were sitting waiting for me.

'Well, here we are,' Hargreaves said, getting up as I arrived. 'Safely back after a nice quiet day. Just keep to the wall and you can't go wrong.' He peered at his watch. 'Tony,' he said, 'they're open. I'll race you down.' They crashed into the dark.

They beat me to the hotel, but dinner had only just finished when I arrived. It was not having anyone to pull me out of the river which really delayed me. I fell in three times before I got the sense to wade about feeling with my hands for a place where I could cross and drag out on my own.

Mr Briggs was kind to me in the morning and put me into the fresh air with some brandy while breakfast was being served. He had ordered a car and asked Blodwen to pack for me as soon as I came down. I don't think I can have looked half as ill as I felt all the same.

Hargreaves came to say good-bye about half past ten. He looked relaxed in a dark suit and a rather nice hat. 'You want to keep away from places like this, Fitzgerald,' he said. 'You really aren't fit enough for it.'

I was allowed to get up two or three weeks later and I came back to P-y-G to finish my convalescence. The first evening someone said: 'The Little Man was here ten days ago. He was asking for you, Kevin. He was sorry to hear you were ill again and said to tell you that he still wasn't awfully fit himself.'

❀ from *Climbers' Club Journal* (1960)

Daloni Seth Hughes | # The Volunteer

The first volunteer for the Milestone Buttress was one of my aunts. She was small and very deaf, but extremely spirited, and as nimble as a goat on the rocks. Her ear trumpet had, of course, to be left at the bottom of the climb, so we arranged to signal to each other by pulls on the rope. It was rather disconcerting, when I gave the rope an accidental tug half-way up a pitch, to hear the gay announcement, 'All right; I'm starting up!'

❋ from *Pinnacle Club Journal* (1934)

J. M. Edwards | A Great Effort

In the last three years three people have asked me how I climb.
Hence this personal article. They said also that it was the state
of mind and not the mechanics that they thought important,
and that if each man would write of himself under this head
then others coming after might know better what to imitate and
what to avoid. A primary condition for this of course would be
to lay aside any modesty that one had at any other times
assumed.

It will be best to describe directly a given instance.

I will not weary you with the preliminaries. There were none.
Everything had been in order, the customary had occurred. I
had come here for the weekend to climb, had got up, dressed,
eaten a good breakfast with a good appetite, and having nobody
to climb with had gone out for the day alone. I had considered
carefully which cliff to visit and chosen a near one not to make
too strenuous a day. This involved walking along a stretch of
road, then a slope up towards the cliff.

The slope I took by stages. Three hundred yards then a rest,
three hundred yards then a rest. During the last war it was
explained to me that the British soldier marched by stages and
it has been my chief method since. It is easier. Some people
prefer to go up hills at a steady ten miles an hour, as if they were
an army tank cruising or Scott hauling sledges in the Antarctic.
I do not. During each rest I gazed at the cliff, exploring from a
distance how a route might go. Then when quite near the cliff
I stopped again and looked up at it more slowly, heavy with the
fresh air, and it looked at me, and it slid about in my eyes as a
cliff sometimes does, and was difficult to focus; I shall go there
and there, I thought, and then perhaps coming to the steeper
portion, I shall go there, or perhaps it will be too hard for me to
go there, then I shall not go there but will go there instead by
what appears so far as can be seen from here to be a dirty and a

bare-sided finger crack, but which may not be so, or otherwise examining the rock closely when we are there, rubbing the nose against it, there may be some third or fourth way, not guessed at from a distance. But first I thought, husbanding my energies I will rest here for a little time where stability can still be assured without effort or trouble by sitting down. So in the middle of the mountains upon a pile of rocks I sat down. A certain tendency to inertia in the mind can have great force.

Do not mistake me, the choice of cliff and of pastime had been free, it was unhampered by any conditions either of expediency or friendship, there was no particular unhappiness on me at this time beyond the normal. Yet I sat down. And as I lifted my head, stones, blocks of rock, sky, cliff faces lay round the field of vision arranged in various ways.

Then later I got up and walked to the foot of the cliff meditating carefully where to start. Then tied the rope on, flung the loose end down the slope and arranged it so that its coils should open without snags. This took some time, due to a complex cluster of small rocks in the way which needed rearranging before I could be sure that the rope would come clean across them. Then I moved on to the rock itself.

Now perhaps you looking on might remark of these actions that none of them had been done in any rapid or decisive mould. You would be right. Perhaps that is why there was no great resultant from them. After twenty minutes I had advanced about fifteen feet and was trembling slightly, not too sure of my position. The rock now before my face was ordinary rock, surfaced at an angle of sixty to seventy degrees, fairly smooth. Heaven was above, the earth a few yards beneath, and I remember nothing of either. As for myself the fore part of my right foot was planted well on a square ledge; the heel overhung into the air and demanded a constant muscular effort at the calf; my left foot was three feet higher and one and a half feet to the side put against a small sloped piece of grooving. In appearance, therefore, had anybody been passing, I was about to step up. In practice I had been trying to do this for ten minutes but had not yet succeeded. It seemed simple, the need was clear, holds were there, but they were small and I am not a man in any way to make a move until satisfied that it is safe, so that to remain in this statuesque and silly position was my only choice for the time being. Every minute or two when my right leg began to tremble I pulled the left leg down from its unserviceable height, bent myself this way and that a little to relieve the strain, then put the leg back again, using the action also as a gesture of purpose.

But any man must be to some degree hard-pressed before he gives up on a point where his heart is set: so I began to struggle. Oh, good heavens, good heavens, I thought, what on earth am I to do, this is not very good, you are being a coward, an arrant coward and this cannot, must not continue, I have time and again pointed out that you are being very silly but you do nothing, you do nothing except stand there with that fixed and ridiculous stare a few feet from the foot of this wretched precipice. But I still accomplished nothing. Then I began to struggle again. I thought, what is wrong, there is something missing, there is no spirit, I am heavy and unable to move; perhaps if I launch out and become sufficiently frightened; in fact I am sure that once over the border there would be no holding me. So I made several attempts to launch out, but nothing happened. Then I thought perhaps if I eat my sandwiches that will improve me, but no, no, for shame, it is not yet half-past eleven, how can I eat them now, yet there can be no harm in it, give yourself a change, I said, eat them all and that will be a load off your mind, then you will not have the temptation to eat again until you get home. So standing still on my footholds and feeling firmer than I had done for some time, I got the tin of sardines out of my pocket, twisted the lid off in the usual way but carefully because of the position, and ate the fish one by one with my mouth. This took some time. Then drained the tin, put it back in my pocket and turned to the rocks once more. Now how will it go, I thought, every excuse is exhausted. And I tried again. No, it is no good, I said, it is no good: here I am fifteen feet from the ground on easy rocks as I said before, it is after lunch but in my own bones there is no more energy than there ever was and my whole soul is as flat as a carpet, what am I to do: perhaps if I were to recall former victories or to picture glory, but how can you do that when you are alone, perhaps if I shouted and sang, but you know you were never able to shout or sing: now if there were an onlooker, that would make an effort worth while: perhaps – is there anyone in sight: no, not a soul, not one in the whole valley: there is no representative of the human race, none to praise, nobody to look surprised at cowardice or to laugh at folly, to provide me with gibe or comparison or stage: there is a sheep, but the sheep do not know about these things, a little bird, but she is away out of sight already. So I stood on waiting, unable to move. It is difficult to describe what it feels like to be so, to describe that extreme desolation that may be left behind in the human brain when it is without anything working in it to spur

it on. I stood on that hold for a long time. Then quickly, with the sweat standing out on my skin and my heart beating, I moved up on to the next holds and then the next and then I did not see what to do and the movement stopped again.

The view had changed. There was heather now in front of my eyes, and some of the thin dust that goes with it. I took a handful of the heather in my right hand. It seemed firm but when bent back it snapped and broke off. A bad material. I made a final effort. Look at yourself, I said, and do you know what this is, that it is schizophrenia, the split mind: I know but I do not care, I said: it is stupid: what could you do if you did get ten feet higher up, the rocks have not started yet to become difficult, take yourself off from this cliff: oh, this climbing, that involves an effort, on every move the holds to be spotted and often there are none, then every limb placed, the body set into the one suitable position found but with trouble, then with the whole organism great force must be exerted, before anything happens, and this to be done while the brain is occupied sick and stiff with its fears: and now you have been doing this for well over an hour and a half and the strain must be telling: get down therefore.

My mind made up, it only remained to go, not always an easy thing to do. But as it has often been remarked God may be merciful, and is so sometimes when you least expect it; and on this occasion it happened that feeling in behind the heather I almost immediately found a good enough spike of rock for my rope and was able to get back down again in no danger. Then I walked a little way up the hillside slowly, rested and walked home.

But the resilience of man is great, and his ingenuity. So I was not done yet and on the way back setting to work I soon picked up my pride in this way, by thinking, today the victory has been to the devil, but tomorrow is not to him yet, also by thinking, it has been said that the secret of life is in detachment from it, good.

❀ from *Climbers' Club Journal* (1941)

anon. | *Verse or Worse*

Been up Snowdon,
A nice ascent.
William Boden
Burton-on-Trent.

❃ from a Visitor's Book in Wales

John Barry | Raven's with the Great Man

We parked by Altnafeadh and bundled out, six of us, in a welter of gear. Then the boot door was hoisted skywards, triggering an avalanche of equipment. The accoutrements of modern ice are awesome. I watched the Great Man with interest – and some nervousness. After all, here in our very midst was one of the *glitterati*, the embodiment of *jeunesse dorée*; and BMC National Officer to boot. We would watch and learn. I knew little about the Man except that he had climbed Everest whilst still a virgin, was reputed to be a nice bloke, and like all nice blokes was popular with grannies.

The five of us waited, respectfully allowing Pete first shot at the mountain of gear that lay strewn half across the A82. If, as I think we did, we expected him to crisply gird himself like some latter-day gladiator we were to be cruelly disappointed. Indeed he paraded woefully ill-equipped, lacklustre even, standing before us sporting not much more than odd stockings, two very pedestrian axes and a supreme indifference to the arsenal which lay all about. 'Don't forget the ropes,' he said and set off toward Great Gully, a painfully thin sack flapping in the wind.

That wind! It was a wild day even down here and Raven's did not look friendly. See it for yourself on one of those raw Rannoch days and you will assuredly agree. This is the Buachaille's bad side; black, malevolent, and the slit of Raven's blacker still. Not friendly. No flirt here with a fine lace of chantilly ice, nor any smile of firmly compliant, sparkling névé beckoning to a summit altar. No, sir. Black walls and a black-eyed gully trapped in a bleak embrace between Slime Wall (what horrors that name conjures for the PA-shod) and Cuneiform Buttress. Hobson's choice. But Raven's was one and we were six, so we had the advantage of her.

Then the wind did for two of them. The wind and an escape ploy that would have graced Patey's pages: 'I live here,' protested

Allan, 'I can afford to wait for better weather. Do it any time.' His partner quickly clipped into the same gambit and they turned with the wind and ran goose-winged back to the car. I envied their sanity, admired their courage, looked askance at Pete. The Great Man, his face set in an expression of frozen insouciance, resolutely plodded on, lugubrious to the last but betraying no sign of the hangover that should have been beheading him while I suffered for all four.

In an hour we gathered at the foot of a gully of steep, soft snow that drowned the first three (summer) pitches and led straight to a chockstone roof which forms the summer crux. Pete surged forward. If I half-expected a Red Sea parting of the powder to allow him unimpeded passage I was, for a second time, disenchanted. The Great Man flailed, grunted and swam – the last a badly co-ordinated butterfly stroke – in a distinctly mortal fashion to collapse in a terrible wrack of panting just below the chockstone. We three followed easily up a well-bulldozed trough. Here Martin Burrows Smith, who instructs these things, suggested that it might be a good thing to rope-up. He joined with Pete, I with Paul Moores.

Pete, now recovered, went at the crux, the wall to the left of the chockstone. It spat him back. Obviously there was even more to Raven's than met the eye. 'My dad did this in 1945 in army boots,' I observed, trying to sound helpful. Whether Pete believed me (and it's true) I have never discovered, but it goaded him to a fury, galvanized him. He charged full frontal to the breech and squeezed up the full 5a of it, axes and crampons sparking where his bludgeon laid bare the rock. The rope ran out at an alarming rate.

I followed, leading my half of the team. It was hard. Jams for the right arm and foot, left axe anxiously searching skyhook incuts. Left front-points despairing a lack of ice, and crampons complaining cacophonous on bare rock. Just when I thought I might be off – downwards – a careless knot in Pete's rope caught between my left front-points and lent me that tiny tug which measures the mile between up and down. Such was the Great Man's surge up the easy slope beyond that he was unaware of his twelve-stone parasite.

I joined him at the mouth of the cave below a second enormous chockstone. It was wilder here. As wild as Smith or Marshall could have ever asked for. Wilder than we wanted, 'wild above rule or art'. The moor had been rough, but this was something else. A vortex of omnidirectional, supersonic spindrift that numbed the senses and stung the flesh. Straight to the vein like Stones' chords or Sibelius's crescendos – go to Raven's on a wild day and you will feel what I mean.

The four of us crawled deeper into the cave and found an eerie haven. Martin produced a flask of coffee, Paul a great nugget of chocolate, I a packet of biscuits. Pete, without so much as a *noblesse oblige*, tucked into all three simultaneously. 'The sports plan is this,' he said at length in superstarspeak, 'there are three or four gigantic chockstones at intervals above this one. With luck they'll all provide a cave just like this. One of you will lead and fix the rope so the rest of us can use it to save time. I've already done the crux for you so you should be OK now. Anyway, I'm a greater-ranges man myself.' Sips of coffee, then 'Now you go first, Paul.'

Paul steeled himself and crawled back to the maelstrom. He had not gone ten feet before we lost sight and sound of him, but thirty seconds later he was back, gasping like a pearl diver:

'What's the problem?' asked Pete, into a mug of coffee.

'Can't breathe out there, or see a thing either.'

'Take a deep breath and just keep going upwards – the line's obvious,' advised Pete through a biscuit. 'And give the rope a couple of tugs when you want us to come up.'

Poor old Paul. He huffed and he puffed and he puffed and he huffed; and he hyperventilated. Then over the top. Pete kicked a dozen coils toward the entrance. 'Enough for him to be going on with.' The minutes ticked by as we chatted comfortably over our coffee and biscuits. From time to time one of us, following the Great Man's example, would foot a few yards of rope to the void, scuttling quickly back to the sanctuary and a sip. 'Much like this on the summit push on the Big "E",' Pete observed casually, adding with equal nonchalance, '28,000 feet higher on Big "E", of course.' Difficult to follow that, and though I struggled for a riposte none came within 20,000 feet.

At last the rope went tight and two tugs signalled an end to our coffee break. Out we went, Somme-style. The weather was daunting; this surely was Armageddon. The wind tore at you. Tore into you. Snatched the breath from between your teeth before you'd barely tasted it. Buffeted the brain insensate and knocked at the heart and challenged: 'Climb me if you dare.' And where or what are you? What pleasures are the draught of this moment? To be sure there's no space, no freedom, no grace or joy in movement. The world ends three inches in front of your face and limbs go where they can, where they will stay – and you seldom see where that is. Can this be the same game that we play in the sun on those slabs a few miles away around the corner? That gambol in shorts with chalk and rubbers? The one a series of narcissistically-deliberate moves, like physical arithmetic; the other a blind, wanton struggle – a gravitational gamble. Can this be the same game? The brain says, 'NO, not at all!' But the soul shouts to be heard – 'Yes it is!'

Martin's turn. Out he goes. Out come the coffee and biscuits. And so we went on. When my turn came I struggled upwards for twenty minutes with little idea where I was until I found myself in the lee of an enormous chasm, 100 feet deep. I cast about, looking for the gully continuation which refused to reveal itself, fixed the ropes and tugged. The others quickly joined me, Pete looking greatly exercised:

'This is the Direct Finish,' he said, 'Chouinard did it. Chimneyed it, and he's even shorter than you.' I didn't believe him. Still don't.

'Got to do something for the second half of your pitch.' The comment chided me down and across left to where I found the groove of the original finish. The climbing was steady, pegs here and there and an occasional glimpse over the left shoulder through the storm to Slime Wall and an evil-looking Shibboleth. A winter ascent of that lot? From the imagination springs such sweet horror! I hugged at my groove and fought back the images that shivered involuntarily across the inward eye, sowing a seed in the sub-conscious. It lingers yet, barren, I hope.

There's a landing fifteen feet from the top, where we joined. Then a convoluted corkscrew of a problem pitch and it's all over. We were out. Out of the vortex, gone from the maelstrom, with nothing worse than the scraich of the wind and a scoot down Great Gully to worry us.

The Great Man spoke and I waited for a leg-pull: 'That's the best day on the hill I've ever had.' His face creased with pleasure and four huge smiles exploded far wider than that Direct Finish. Raven's had beaten badinage.

POSTSCRIPT

I wrote this on the bus coming back from Chamonix. A few minutes after I had put down that last full stop we pulled into Victoria where I bought a newspaper. Peter Boardman, it told me, was dead on Everest. Stricken, I returned to this story and hacked at all that now seemed in bad taste. Daft, of course, but understandable, I hope. Most of it is back now, as it should be. As he would have asked.

The sad thing is that he had wanted to write about Raven's for this book. It was his best day on the hill, he repeated. I refused to budge for reasons I can scarcely admit even to myself. If only I had.

I wish that this were a story of such merit as to match Pete's best day, a best story for his best day. Alas, the gift is not mine to give. But it was a great day on a fine climb with a great mate – and a marvellous memory.

❧ from *Cold Climbs* (1983)

We were close friends and that friendship was based on badinage – our Anglo-Saxon backgrounds allowing nothing outwardly closer. I recall a fatuous argument we had one day while stumbling up the Allt a' Mhuilinn about the importance of physical courage (of which he had more than most). I loosed off schoolboy Kipling, Henry V and Graves. Pete's counters were weightier by far: Grass, Eliot, Lawrence, until the CIC Hut brought a truce. Then a climb consumed our energies.

Well, I could never make much sense of your writing team, Pete, so in Kipling's words, 'Here's my best respects to you.'

❧ *John Barry* (1984)

J. B. Morton | *Nature Lover*

On the moors the plover cried: and the sound is like the creaking of a badly oiled door. Let the ornithologists put that in their snares and smoke it. Also a bird with a call like a falsetto whinny, and a very long nose, rose from a hummock at my feet and made the day hideous with its noise.

C. E. Montague | *In Hanging Garden Gully*

To climb up rocks is like all the rest of your life, only simpler
and safer. In all the rest of your life, any work you may do, by
way of a trade, is a taking of means to some end. That end may
be good. We all hope it is. But who can be sure? Misgiving is
apt to steal in. Are you a doctor – is it your job to keep all the
weak ones alive? Then are you not spoiling the breed for the
future? Are you a parson or politician or some sort of public
improver, always trying to fight evil down? May you not then
be making a muff every day of somebody else who ought to
have had his dragon to fight, with his own bow and spear, when
you rushed in to rob him and the other little St Georges of
discipline and of victory? Anyhow, all the good ends seem a
good long way off, and the ways to them dim. You may be old
by the time you are there. The salt may have lost half its savour.

No such dangers or doubts perplex the climber on rocks. He
deals, day by day, with the Ultimate Good, no doubt in small
nips, but still authentic and not watered down. His senses thrill
with delight to find that he is just the sum of his own simple
powers. He lives on, from moment to moment, by early man's
gleeful achievement of balance on one foot out of four. He hangs
safe by a single hand that learnt its good grip in fifty thousand
years of precarious dodging among forest boughs, with the
hungry snakes looking up from the ground for a catch, like the
expectant fieldsmen in the slips. The next little ledge, the object
of all human hope and desire, is only some twelve feet away –
about the length of the last leap of that naked bunch of clenched
and quivering muscles, from whom you descend, at the wild
horse that he had stalked through the grass. Each time that you
get up a hard pitch you have succeeded in life. Besides, no one
can say you have hurt him.

Care will come back in the end: the clouds return after the
rain; but for those first heavenly minutes of sitting secure and

supreme at the top of Moss Ghyll or the Raven Crag Gully you
are Columbus when he saw land from the rigging and Gibbon
when he laid down his pen in the garden-house at Lausanne.
It's good for you, too; it makes you more decent. No one, I firmly
believe, could be utterly mean on the very tip of the Weisshorn.
I could, if I had known the way, have written a lyric about these
agreeable truths as I sat by myself in the tiny inn at Llyn Ogwen,
where Telford's great London-to-Holyhead road climbs over a
pass between three-thousand-foot Carnedds and Glyders. I was
a convalescent then, condemned still to a month of rest cure for
body and mind. But it was June, and fine weather. Rocks had
lately become dry and warm.

There are places in Britain where rock-climbing cannot hon-
estly be called a rest cure. I mean, for the body. Look at the
Coolin – all the way that a poor invalid must tramp from
Sligachan southward before he gets among the rough, trusty,
prehensile gabbro, the best of all God's stones. Think of Scafell
Crag, the finest crag in the world, but its base cut off from the
inn by all that Sisyphean plod up the heart-breaking lengths of
Brown Tongue. From Ogwen you only need walk half an hour,
almost on the flat, and then – there you are, at the foot of your
climb. The more I considered the matter, the more distinctly
could I perceive that my doctor, when saying 'Avoid all violent
exercise' meant that if ever I got such an opening as this for a
little 'steady six-furlong work', as it is called in the training
reports, I ought to take care not to miss it.

But I was the only guest at the inn. And to climb alone is
counted a sin against the spirit of the sport. All the early fathers
of climbing held the practice heretical. Certainly some of them
– Whymper, Tyndall, and others – climbed by themselves when
they had a mind to. Thus did King David, on distinguished
occasions, relax the general tensity of his virtue. But these
exceptions could not obscure the general drift of .   ɔw and the
prophets of mountaineering. Then came another pause-giving
reflection. If, as the Greeks so delicately put it, anything
incurable happens while you are climbing alone, your clay is
exposed, defenceless and dumb, to nasty *obiter dicta* during the
inquest. 'Woe unto him', as Solomon says, 'who is alone when
he falleth!' Insensate rustic coroners and juries, well as they may

understand that riding to hounds in a stone-wall country is one of the choicer forms of prudence, will prose and grumble over extinct mountaineers. Their favourite vein is the undesirable one of their brother, the First Clown in *Hamlet*, who thought it a shame that Ophelia (she seems to have slipped up while climbing a tree) 'should have countenance in this world to drown or hang herself, more than her even Christian'.

No mean impediments these to a sensitive, conscientious nature's design for seeking health and joy among the attractive gullies and slabs that surround Llyn Idwal. Against them I marshalled all that I could remember of St Paul's slighting observations on the law; also any agility that I had gained in the Oxford Greats school in resolving disagreeable discords into agreeable higher harmonies. Black was certainly not white. Still, as the good Hegelian said, black might, after all, be an aspect of white. In time it was duly clear to my mind that sin lies not in the corporal act, but in the thoughts of the sinner. So long as the heart sincerely conversed with the beauty of the truths on which rested the rule of never climbing alone it mattered little what the mere legs did: your soul was not in your legs. One of casuistry's brightest triumphs had been fairly won, my liberty gained, my intellectual integrity saved, my luncheon sandwiches ordered for eight in the morning – when somebody else arrived at the inn.

He stood confessed a botanist – he had the large green cylindrical can of the tribe, oval in section and hung by a strap from the shoulder, like the traditional *vivandière*'s little cask in French art. He was also, I found while we smoked through that evening together, a good fellow. He had, too, a good leg, if one only. The other was stiff and unbendable at the knee. He had broken it last year, he said, and the bones seemed to have set only too hard, or else Nature had gracelessly grudged to the mended knee-joint of her lover a proper supply of whatever substitute she uses for ball-bearings.

His name was Darwin. 'No relation, really,' he humbly assured me. His father was only some obscure squire. The son's Christian name had been Charles at the font, but on coming of age the dear fellow had felt it immodest to prey any more than he need upon his eponymous hero's thrice-honoured names. So he had meekly converted the Charles by deed-poll into Thomas. This lowly and beautiful gesture convinced me, as you may suppose, that here was the man to go climbing with. He was indeed one of the innocent, one-thoughted kind that wake up happy each day and never turn crusty, and always think you are being too good to them.

One lure alone had drawn him to these outworks of Snowdon. Some eccentric flower grew on these heights, and a blank page in one of his books of squashed specimens ached for it. Was it so lovely? I asked, like a goose. He was too gentle to snub me. But all that fellow's thoughts shone out through his face. Every flower that blew – to this effect did his soul mildly rebuke mine – was beauteous beyond Helen's eyes. All he said was: 'No, not fair, perhaps, to outward view as many roses be; but, just think! – it grows on no patch of ground in the world but these crags!'

'It is not merely better dressed,' said I, 'than Solomon. It is wiser.'

It was about then, I think, that the heart of the man who had gone mad on the greenstuff and that of the man who knew what was what, in the way of a recreation, rushed together like Paolo's and Francesca's. What had already become an *entente cordiale* ripened at tropical speed into alliance. Darwin had found a second, half invalided perhaps, but still the holder of two unqualified legs, for tomorrow's quest of his own particular Grail. To me it now seemed to be no accident that Darwin had come to the inn: it was ordained, like the more permanent union of marriage, for a remedy against sin, and to avoid climbing alone.

We got down to business at once. A charming gully, I told him, led right up to the big crag over Cwm Idwal. Not Twll Du, the ill-famed Devil's Kitchen. That, I frankly said, was justly *detestata matribus* – wet and rotten and lethal, and quite another affair. Mine was the place for town children to spend a happy day in the country: the very place also for starting the day's search for the object of Darwin's desire. In saying this, too, I was honest. Lots of plants grow in some gullies; ferns, mosses, grasses, all sorts of greens flourish in a damp cleft, like hair in an armpit; why not one kind of waste rabbit-food as well as another? You see, I had not been a casuist merely, before Darwin came. I had used the eyes heaven gave me, and reconnoitred the gully well from below, and if any flower knew how to tell good from bad, in the way of a scramble, it would be there. I ended upon a good note. The place's name, I said impressively, was Hanging Garden Gully, no doubt because of the rich indigenous flora.

His eyes shone at that, and we went straight to the kitchen to ask Mrs Jones for the loan of a rope. I had none with me that journey: the sick are apt to relinquish improvidently these necessaries of a perfect life. Now, in the classics of mountaineering the right thing in such cases of improvised enterprise is that the landlady lends you her second-best clothes-line. Far happier we, Mrs Jones having by her a 120-foot length of the right Alpine rope, with the red worsted thread in its middle. It had been left in her charge by a famous pillar of the Scottish Mountaineering Club till he should come that way again. 'The gentleman,' Mrs Jones told us, 'said I was always to let any climbing gentlemen use it.' Heaven was palpably smiling upon our attempt.

The sun smiled benedictively, too, on the halt and the sick as they stood, about nine the next morning, roping up at the foot of their climb. 'A fisherman's bend,' I took care to explain, as I knotted one end of the rope round Darwin's chest.

'The botanical name,' he replied – 'did I tell you? – is Lloydia.' How some men do chatter when they are happy! Can't carry their beans.

We were not likely to need the whole 120 feet of the rope. So I tied myself on at its middle and coiled the odd sixty feet round my shoulder. 'A double overhand knot,' I confessed, as I tightened it round me. 'A bad knot, but for once it may do us no harm.'

'The vernacular name,' said the garrulous fellow, 'is spider-wort.'

'Tut, tut!' I inwardly said.

The lower half of that gully was easier than it had looked: just enough in it to loosen your muscles and make you want more. Higher up, the gully grew shallow and had greater interest. The top part of all, as I remember it now, might be called either a chimney or crack, being both. In horizontal section it was a large obtuse angle indented into the face of the crag. The crag at this part, and the gully's bed with it, rose at an angle of some sixty degrees. Now when you climb rock at an angle of sixty degrees the angle seems to be just ninety. In early mountaineering records the pioneers often say, 'Our situation was critical. Above us the crag rose vertical', or 'To descend was impossible now. But in front the rocky face, for some time perpendicular, had now begun to overhang'. If you take a clinometer to the scenes of some of those liberal estimates you blush for your kind. The slope of the steepest – and easiest – ridge of the three by which the Matterhorn is climbed is only thirty-nine degrees. But this, though not purely digressive, is partly so. All that strictly had to be said was that an upright and very obtuse-angled trough in smooth rock that rises at sixty degrees cannot be climbed.

But in the very bed of our trough there had been eroded, from top to bottom, a deepish irregular crack in the rock. Into this crack, at most parts, you could stick a foot, a knee, or an arm. Also, the sides of the large obtuse angle, when you looked closely, were not utterly smooth. On the right wall, as we looked up, certain small wrinkles, bunions, and other minute but lovable diversities in the face of the stone gave promise of useful points of resistance for any right boot that might scrape about on the wall in the hope of exerting auxiliary lateral pressure, while the left arm and thigh, hard at work in the crack, wriggled you up by a succession of caterpillarish squirms. This delectable passage was eighty feet high, as I measured it with my experienced eye. An inexperienced measuring-tape might have put it at fifty. To any new recruit to the cause – above all, to one with a leg as inflexible as the stoniest stone that it pressed – I felt that the place was likely to offer all that he could wish in the line of baptisms of fire. Still, as the pioneers said, to descend was impossible now: the crack was too sweet to be left. And Darwin, thus far, had come up like a lamplighter, really. I told him so, frankly. Alpine guides are the men at psychology. Do they not get the best out of the rawest new client, in any hard place, by ceasing to hide the high estimate that they have formed of his natural endowment for the sport? *'Vous êtes – je vous dis franchement, monsieur – un chamois! Un véritable chat de montagne!'*

I was leading the party. I was the old hand. Besides, I could bend both my knees. Desiring Darwin to study my movements, so that he presently might – so far as conformity would not cramp his natural talents – copy them closely, I now addressed myself to the crack. When half-way up I heard the voice of a good child enduring with effort, a painful call upon its patience. 'Any Lloydia yet?' it wistfully said. Between my feet I saw Darwin below. Well, he was certainly paying the rope out all right, as I had enjoined; but he did it 'like them that dream'. His mind was not in it. All the time he was peering hungrily over the slabby containing walls of the gully, and now he just pawed one of them here and there with a tentative foot – you know how a puppy, when first it sees ice, paws the face of the pond. 'These botanists!' I thought. 'These fanatics!' You know how during a happy physical effort – a race or a hunt, a fight or a game – you think, with a sort of internal quiet, about a lot of old things. There came back to my mind the old lines that I had once had to make Latin verse of:

> How vainly men themselves amaze
> To win the palm, the oak, or bays,
> And their incessant labours see
> Crowned from some single herb or tree.

Meanwhile I took a precaution. I first unroped myself. Then I passed the rope, from below, through the space behind a stone that was jammed fast in the crack. Then I roped myself on again, just at my old place on the rope. A plague of a job it was, too, with all those sixty feet of spare rope to uncoil and re-coil. But you see how it worked: I had now got the enthusiast moored. Between him and me the rope went through the eye of a needle, so I could go blithely on. I went. In the top of the crack I found a second jammed stone. It was bigger than number one: in fact, it blocked the way and made you clamber round outside it rather interestingly; but it, too, had daylight showing through a hole behind it. Sounds from below were again improving my natural stock of prudence. You can't, I thought, be too safe. Once more I unroped, just under this chockstone, and pushed the rope up through the hole at its back. When the rope fell down to me, outwards over the top of the stone, I tied on again, just as before, and then scrambled up over the outer side of the stone with an ecstatic pull on both arms, and sat on its top in the heaven that big-game hunters know when they lie up against the slain tiger and smoke.

If you have bent up your mind to take in the details, you will now have an imposing vision of the connections of Darwin and me with each other and with the Primary or Palaeozoic rocks of Cambria. From Darwin, tied on to its end, the rope ran, as freely as a bootlace runs through the eyelets, behind the jammed stone thirty feet above his head, and then again behind my present throne of glory at the top; then it was tied on to me; and then there were sixty feet, half its length, left over to play with.

Clearly Darwin, not being a thread, or even a rope, could not come up the way that the rope did, through the two needle-eyes. Nor did I care, he being the thing that he was, to bid him untie and then to pull up his end of the rope through the eyes, drop it down to him clear through the air, and tell him to tie on again. He was, as the Irish say of the distraught, 'fit to be tied', and not at all fit for the opposite. If he were loose he might at any moment espy that Circe of his in some place out of bounds. There seemed to be only one thing to do. I threw down the spare sixty feet of the rope, and told him first to tie himself on to its end, and then, but not before, to untie himself from the other. I could not quite see these orders obeyed. A bulge of rock came between him and my eyes, but I was explicit. 'Remember that fisherman's bend!' I shouted. Perhaps my voice was rather austere; but who would not forgive a wise virgin for saying, a little dryly, to one of the foolish, 'Well, use your spare can'? As soon as he sang out 'All right' I took a good haul on what was now the working half of the rope, to test his knot-making. Yes, he *was* all right. So I bade him come up, and he started. Whenever he looked up I saw that he had a wild, gadding eye; and whenever he stopped to breathe during the struggle he gasped, 'I can't see it yet.'

He came nearly half-way, and then he did see it. He had just reached the worst part. Oh, the Sirens know when to start singing! That flower of evil was far out of his reach, or of what his reach ought to have been. Some twelve feet away on his right it was rooted in some infinitesimal pocket of blown soil, a

'Then he left all and made for his Hero.'

mere dirty thumbnailful of clay. For a moment the lover eyed
the beloved across one huge slab of steep stone with no real
foothold or handhold upon it – only a few efflorescent minutiae
small as the bubukles and whelks and knobs on the nose of
some fossil Bardolph. The whole wall of the gully just there was
what any man who could climb would have written off as
unclimbable. Passion, however, has her own standards, beyond
the comprehension of the wise:

> His eye but saw that light of love,
> The only star it hailed above.

My lame Leander gave one whinny of desire. Then he left all and
made for his Hero.

You know the way that a man, who has no idea how badly he
bats, will sometimes go in and hit an unplayable bowler right
out of the ground, simply because the batsman is too green to
know that the bowler cannot be played. Perhaps that was the

way. Or perhaps your sound climber, having his wits, may leave, at his boldest, a margin of safety, as engineers call it, so wide that a madman may cut quite a lot off its edge without coming surely to grief. Or was it only a joke of the gods among themselves over their wine? Or can it be that the special arrangements known to be made for the safety of sailors, when in their cups, are extended at times to cover the case of collectors overcome by the strong waters of the acquisitive instinct? Goodness knows! Whatever the powers that helped him, this crippled man, who had never tried climbing before, went skating off to his right flank, across that impossible slant, on one foot and one stilt, making a fool of the science of mountaineering.

I vetoed, I imprecated, I grew Athanasian. All utterly useless. As soon could you whistle a dog back to heel when he fleets off on fire with some fresh amour. I could only brace myself, take a good hold of the rope in both hands, and be ready to play the wild salmon below as soon as he slipped and the line ran out tight. While I waited I saw, for the first time, another piquant detail of our case. Darwin, absorbed in his greed, had never untied the other end of the rope. So he was now tied on to both ends. The whole rope made a circle, a vicious circle. Our whole caravan was sewn on to the bony structure of Wales with two big stitches, one at each jammed stone.

You see how it would work. When Darwin should fall, as he must, and hang in the air from my hands, gravitation would swing him back into the centre of the chimney, straight below me, bashing him hard against the chimney's opposite wall. No doubt he would be stunned. I should never be able to hoist his dead weight through the air to my perch, so I should have to lower him to the foot of the chimney. That would just use up the full sixty feet of rope. It would run the two sixty-foot halves of the rope so tight that I should never be able to undo the bad central knot that confined me. Could I but cut it when Darwin was lowered into provisional safety, and then climb down to see him! No; I had lost my knife two days ago. I should be like a netted lion, with no mouse to bite through his cords: a Prometheus, bound to his rock.

But life spoils half her best crises. That wretch never slipped.

He that by this time had no sort of right to his life came back as he went, treading on air, but now with that one bloom of the spiderwort in his mouth. Apologizing for slowness, and panting with haste, he writhed up the crack till his head appeared over the chockstone beside me. Then he gave one cry of joy, surged up over the stone, purring with pleasure, and charged the steep slope of slippery grass above the precipice we had scaled. 'You never told me!' he cried; and then for the first time I noticed that up here the whole place was speckled with Lloydia. The next moment Darwin fell suddenly backwards as if Lloyd himself or some demon gardener of his had planted a very straight one on the chin of the onrushing trespasser in his pleasaunce. You guess? Yes. One of his two tethers, the one coming up from behind the lower jammed stone, had run out; it had pulled him up short as he leapt upon the full fruition of his desire.

He was easy to field as he rolled down the grass. But his tug on the rope had worked it well into some crevice between the lower jammed stone and the wall of the crack. We were anchored now, good and fast, to that stone, more than three fathoms below. What to do now? Climb down and clear the jammed rope? Leave that lame voluptuary rioting upon a precipice's edge? Scarcely wise – would it have been? Puzzled and angry, I cast away shame. I knew well that as Spartan troops had to come back with their shields or upon them, or else have trouble with their mothers, a climber who leaves his tackle behind in a retreat is likely to be a scorn and a hissing. Still, I cast away shame. Ours was no common case; no common ethics would meet it. I untied us both, and threw both ends of the rope down the chimney; then I let Darwin graze for a minute; then I drove him relentlessly up the steep grass to the top of the crag, and round by the easy walking way down.

As we passed down the valley below I looked up. The whole length of our chimney was visibly draped with the pendant double length of that honest Scots mountaineer's rope. 'I don't really know how to thank you enough,' Darwin was babbling beside me, 'for giving me such a day!'

But I felt as if I were one of the villains in plays who compromise women of virtue and rank by stealing their fans and leaving them lying about in the rooms of bad bachelors. Much might be said for climbing alone, no matter what the authorities thought. A good time it would be, all to myself, when I came back to salvage that rope.

❀ from *Fiery Particles* (1923)

G. D. Abraham | *Weather Report*

All British mountain districts are notorious for rainy weather.
An old Cumbrian was once met by a tourist after a week of
persistent rain and asked if it ever did anything but rain there.
'Yaas!' answered the dry old dalesman; 'it sometimes snaws!'

❧ from *British Mountain Climbs* (1909)

Peter Graves | A Day with the Angel

It was one of those hot summers of the mid-sixties. Remember them? Ah, youth. This particular hot summer (there was more than one of them) the Angel and I were doing the Moor in a lazy sort of way. Day here, day there, few pints here, more there; picking the plums, so to speak. Central Groove at the Dewerstone, full of horrible hard Marines shouting obscenities at reluctant recruits who had never known that the Army was going to be like this. Sarcophagus and Wogs at Chudleigh, Patey-type perfection in a rural paradise at the wrong end of the country. So to Hay Tor, where we entertained the tourists and terrified ourselves on Vandal and Ann. Oh, the roundedness! Who was the small boy in welly boots who followed us half-way up the first pitch encouraged by a manifestly lunatic male parent? 'Go on, Jimmy, show 'em. Ee, what a lad that Jimmy is!' Jimmy is presumably dead or dead hard by now, possibly both.

We retired to the Rock Inn to rest our arms. Is it possible to feel out of place in the snug corner of a bijou beamed bar in a Devon pub? Yes. Perhaps it was the rusting van we left outside or the odour of having slept in the said van that we took inside. Or the CND badges. (Remember when every aspiring hardy was an ardent disarmer?) We ignored the other occupants. The women were Vogue-ish, not enough flesh on them; the men straight from a fresh-air ad. for menthol cigarettes. They all looked so clean. There has to be something wrong with people who look that clean. We agreed on athlete's foot and fetched another pint, trying to appear suavely rugged rather than dirty. The expression on Mine Host's face told us that he was not getting the message, so we did the surly proletarian act instead. We were nothing if not adaptable.

I should tell you about me and the Angel. The grammar is his and no doubt he is now teaching it as the correct form to a whole generation of children. They in turn probably spend their entire energy on goading him into using one of the many expletives which make up his basic vocabulary.

As I said, all this happened a long time ago, just about the time gear was becoming trendy. Before that, given a pair of boots and a rope you were away. But about the mid-sixties Brigham, Brown, Black and the rest got hold of the paperback on 'The Affluent Society' and decided that the bands of tatty bogies native to the British hills had pennies in their pouches. Pennies that were being wasted on beer and worse. Pennies that needed redistributing according to the capitalist ethic. So out came the colour catalogues to fill our winter nights with envy. Breeches well-filled by beautiful birds, caggies worn by craggy-jawed men staring at a distant horizon with not a hair out of place, Kernmantel, clogs, bongs and boots of guaranteed Outer Mongolian camel hide. At a price. In short, they gave us an image. At a price.

Me and the Angel wanted that image but in no way were we about to redistribute our pennies. The brewers were relying on us. We tried psychological self-deception. What was good enough for Haskett-Smith was good enough for us. Anyway, the trendies were a bunch of poofters, weren't they? No good. We still wanted that image. So we cut corners, which is why two figures could be seen treading the hills in hand-sewn cagoules, home-knitted Norwegian socks (grandmothers have their uses), one tape-sling and a lot of old rope ones, one PA crab and a lot of old Stubais. Plus all the nuts from a clapped-out Ford Popular on the local tip. Man, we felt great. Maybe it was only half an image but it was half-price. We even had crash hats and that was very IN. People thought you had been to the Alps. It was the Angel's hat that always drew attention, and gave him his name. He had bought it off a motor-cycling acquaintance who wasn't going to need it for a year, having been found struggling under the burden of a hundredweight of somebody else's lead. Lovingly painted around the rim were seventeen swastikas; red lettering across the dome announced 'Angel of Death'. By comparison my hat was a modest affair, white and peaked, previously owned by a lady scooterist with buck teeth. All of which possibly explains the scene in the Rock Inn.

We had a third pint and decided to do Raven Gully on Low

Man. The old guide called it V. Diff., the new one called it Severe, but both agreed that it is one of the best things on the Moor. A hundred feet in three short pitches and just the thing to start a warm, lazy afternoon. Back we went through the sandwich eaters around Hay Tor and down to Low Man, which the tourists only find by falling over it. The time: 2.30; the weather: very hot; the climb: a forty-foot triangular slab started by a layback move, followed by twenty feet of overhanging chimney and finishing with forty feet of easy blocks. Up in no time.

The Angel offered to lead the first pitch and before I had time to start the usual argument of principle he was off bearing with him the tape-sling, the P A crab and half a hundredweight of rusty Ford Popular. He was always trying to muscle in on the full image at my expense; you have to look out for yourself in this game. Carrying all that gear made him feel good and he put on a show of delicate slab work, all lithe movement and televisual posture, even though the holds were big enough to take your granny up. Every five feet he slotted in a little piece of Ford Popular, hub nuts and the like. Very professional-looking until you realized that he had to get rid of some of the stuff because the weight of it was throttling him. The only sound was the gentle sloshing of the beer in his belly as he moved. Five minutes and he was up and tying himself into a triangular niche at the bottom of the chimney. 'Nice little pitch,' he muttered just loud enough for me to hear. It was the signal for me to praise his style but I said nothing. Let him polish his own ego. My turn. I took it coolly as a demonstration of how these things should really be done. Most of my time was spent removing the pieces of automobile with which he had littered the route.

At 2.45 I reached him, and that was when the trouble started. One thing about the Angel is his size: it's big. It's also gangly with a knack of finding the most inconvenient positions – for others. Sitting alone he can make a railway compartment impenetrable with a jungle of arms and legs; sitting on a small stance he can double the grade of the route. I was trying to lead through. 'Masses of holds,' said the Angel, covering all of them with his bulk. 'Masses. Big ones too.' Abuse was exchanged but the man was immovable, fixed to the rock, with an idiot grin below his coronet of swastikas. At three o'clock I was level with his head and spread in a trouser-splitting straddle; fifteen minutes later I was six feet higher and in the same uncomfortable position but now coughing from the industrial filth of chain-smoked Woodies on the stance below. All this to a mixed accompaniment of encouragement, sage advice, giggles and indecent comment.

Then there was the overhanging chimney – so called. More a wide crack, really, pushing out and leaning left. The answer was to ignore it, get out on the left wall and climb it straight. But I couldn't. The Angel had blocked the approach and anyway it looked airy out there. So I would have to thrutch it, and soon, as the straddle was becoming painful and the sundry pieces of Ford picked up on the way were getting heavy. I found something large for my left hand and heaved in an attempt to get my right leg nearer my left.

The proverb should run 'Look before you heave – especially in overhanging cracks.' But I had not. There was a thud. The peaked helmet, once the pride of a buck-toothed scooterist, jammed tight in the crack and my head jammed tight and immovable in the helmet. That was at 3.30. Safe as houses. I had four points of contact with the rock: one jammed head, one large and one small handhold, one medium foothold and the other leg thrashing about in space like a string puppet. Movement up was prevented by the helmet, movement down by the chin-strap on which I began to rely more and more for support as the inevitable leg and arm shake set in. The ninety minutes' struggle to undo the chin-strap need not be described in detail. It's enough to say that, whenever I removed my right hand from its hold to reach the strap, the leftward lean and overhanging nature of the crack caused me to pivot on my one foothold. The pivoting in turn caused my neck to be screwed in a manner unpleasantly like the death of a farmyard hen. At 4.45 I won and collapsed completely exhausted on the large ledge above the chimney, having left the helmet stuck there like a large white chock.

But meantime what of the Angel? His initial amazement rapidly changed to malicious mirth. I had been able to hear him the whole time. Roars of laughter were interspersed with unprintable abuse and snatches of 'He's just a puppet on a chin' rendered in a voice cracked by nicotine addiction. Joyfully, he estimated the length of the impending fall, noted the abrasive quality of the rock I would pass on my way, doubted his own ability to hold me and offered moronic advice on how to make my descent less painful. He even made my will for me and suggested passing it up on an empty cigarette packet for my signature. Occasionally, by swivelling my sweating eyeballs through ninety degrees, I could see him snugly tucked in his niche, tears of pleasure rolling out under his National Health glasses and making a few clean streaks on his otherwise grubby face. And always that red slogan on his helmet – Angel of Death. Who needs friends?

Ten minutes lying flat and trembling on the ledge above the chimney gave me enough energy to think of revenge. I ran the rope through a crab and sling attached to an immense chock and winched in the slack until roars of discomfort from below assured me that the Angel was being stretched breathless between the rope and his belay slings. Then I tied it off, soloed the easy last pitch and retired to the Rock Inn.

from *Climber and Rambler* (1975)

Showell Styles | # The Climber's Clementine

Air,
'Clementine'

On a Clogwyn, close to Ogwen,
  Where the clouded cliffs incline,
Clung a climber, fine old-timer,
  And his daughter, Clementine.

> *Chorus*:
>   O my darling, O my darling,
>   O my climbing Clementine,
>   Thou art lost and gone forever,
>   Dreadful sorry, Clementine!

She was leading, like a fairy,
  On a hundred feet of line,
While her father, nervous rather,
  Fast belayed his Clementine.

From the cliff top I was watching,
  Thinking, O that she were mine!
She's so love-ly from above-ly,
  Is my climbing Clementine!

Saw her groping, vainly hoping,
  For a handhold mighty fine;
But alack, there was no crack there,
  To support my Clementine.

Then the climber, fine old-timer,
  Anxious for his Clementine,
Shouted 'Hi, sir! You up there, sir!
  Can't you drop my girl a line?'

Quick as thought I hitched my nylon
  To a belay crystalline,
Standing firm as any pylon,
  Dropped the rope to Clementine.

And she grasped it, swiftly clasped it
  Round her slender waist divine;
Up I drew her quite secu-er,
  So I saved my Clementine.

Then she rose up, cocked her nose up,
  With a glance that chilled my spine.
'I'd no need, sir, on that lead, sir,
  Of your help,' said Clementine.

So I parted, broken-hearted,
  From the dreams that once were mine;
Gave all hope up, coiled the rope up,
  Said goodbye to Clementine.

Then the climber, fine old-timer,
  Stood me lots and lots of wine –
Now I'd rather climb with father
  Than his haughty Clementine!

❀ from *The Mountaineer's Week-End Book* (1950)

Tom Patey | The Aiguille Bonington

The last day of the holiday found us on the road for the Storr Rocks. We had been assured by several climbers that the rock here was no better than porridge, but with a distrust born of long association with rival scalp hunters we had been forced to investigate the place for ourselves. We could now confirm the accuracy of their reports. The rock is like porridge – in consistency though not quality, for porridge is a part of our national heritage and a feast fit for a king. This was not.

Nevertheless it is a weird, fascinating spot, almost Dolomitic in contour. The rock is perhaps at its best on the Old Man of Storr and even there is dangerously loose. Don Whillans, who led the only recorded ascent of the Old Man two years ago, would be surprised to hear that local tradition credits the feat to a thirteen-year-old American lass who is reputed to have nipped up and down in her plimsolls. The date is not specified but it may be assumed that no pitons were used. It is also rumoured that the Devil lives on the summit.

One hundred yards to the north of the Old Man is another pinnacle, overshadowed by its neighbour yet from some angles even more bizarre. Daylight can be seen through three ragged windows in the crumbling masonry, suggesting a fanciful resemblance to a ruined cathedral. The topmost spire looked as if it might yield to a strong push.

'How about that!' I cried enthusiastically.

'Very picturesque,' Bonington commented briefly.

'I mean, as a route.' He sat up.

'Now why should anyone want to climb a heap of disintegrating rubbish like that? You tell me.'

Here was my cue.

'Because it is there,' I answered (recalling an apt phrase from a climbing book).

For this was no insignificant mole-hill. It was a virgin summit,

modest by Alpine or even Cuillin proportions but nevertheless a potential Aiguille Bonington or Sgùrr Tom. We took the rope as an afterthought and lived to be grateful. After a scramble of 100 feet we came out on to the *arête* opposite the Old Man and had to readjust our scale of dimensions. There was still seventy-five feet to climb and it was not easy. We split it into three pitches in order to limit the momentum of any loose rock dislodged by the leader. A crash helmet would have been useful for the second.

At last, after a titanic struggle, Chris balanced delicately on the topmost block and performed the time-honoured summit rites. It then occurred to him that the descent might present its own special problems. He would not consider climbing down by the same route and there was nowhere to fix a *rappel* rope. It was all very depressing. His only hope lay in adjusting the rope across the very tip of the pinnacle so that I could lower him down to safety, but the manoeuvre was fraught with danger for two very obvious reasons. In the first place the rope might slip from its moorings: again, and more important from my point of view, the whole top of the pinnacle might break off under the extra strain. In the event nothing untoward occurred – otherwise I would not have lived to tell the tale – but it left me with an acute attack of the 'heeby-jeebies'.

It is tempting to consider how ironic it might have been for Bonington to have achieved the pinnacle of his desire only to be marooned there for all time. One pictures a statuesque yet almost absurd figure sitting cross-legged on its lofty pedestal, contemplating the passing crowds with a jaundiced eye and being fed periodically from a long pole. In climbing circles it would have perpetuated for all time the fame of the Aiguille Bonington and for the tourist trade would have been an unexpected fillip – perhaps an even greater attraction than the Loch Ness Monster! Who knows? Alas for the historian, ' 'tis of such stuff that dreams are made'. Miracles never happen in real life – only in fairy-tales.

🌸 from 'Over the Sea to Skye', *Etchachan Club Journal* (1962)

Walt Unsworth | 'But I Don't Want to be Rescued!'

It was not the sort of day you thought about rescue really. It was one of those glorious days you sometimes get at Easter on the Ben when the sky arcs clear blue over the glistening white mountains, and you want to be up and away, out of the homely squalor of the CIC Hut and on to the hill.

At least, that's how Ed Adamson and I felt about it, though our companion, a young man who answered to the name of Tash for some improbable reason, thought differently. Tash lived entirely off a diet of fish and chips and hot meat pies, and since such luxuries seldom appear on the CIC Hut menu, Tash was losing energy fast. He elected to stay at the hut in the hope that he would still have enough strength left at the end of the holiday to enable him to stagger down at least as far as the chippy in Fort Bill.

I forget what Ed and I did that day, but I know we had an enjoyable time and as the sun began to set, we skittered down No. 4 Gully and back to the hut.

Tash was sitting there, conserving energy, but no longer alone. In one of the bunks lay a pale-faced young man sipping coffee. Well, the walk up the Allt a' Mhuilinn has that effect on some people, but Tash had a strange tale to relate.

It seems that earlier in the day the young man and his wife had strolled up the Allt a' Mhuilinn from Fort William out of sheer curiosity. They were in fact on their honeymoon, so it was obvious the lad was not without stamina. Finding the CIC Hut they had called in on Tash and asked his advice about continuing further and he had advised them not to bother; not in high-heeled shoes and a double-breasted suit, anyway. As he pointed out, it wasn't really the right gear for the Ben.

But the couple were not to be so easily thwarted. Put off the Ben they turned their attention to the great shaly slopes of Carn Mor Dearg opposite. Now, I don't know whether you know these slopes but they consist of granular crap set at a critical angle; probably the only slopes in Britain likely to avalanche *before* it snows. In hard snow they give splendid glissades but when the snow is patchy or thawing they are purgatory. It was thawing that day, and the upshot was that a boulder rolled over and broke the young man's ankle.

Well, they staggered back to the hut, where Tash was still quietly conserving energy. A crisis was imminent. It looked as though he would have to expend energy by taking the woman down to Fort William whilst her newly acquired husband sat it out in the hut, though Tash could have called at the chippy whilst he was there, of course. However, this was not to be, for at the crucial moment two more tourists had appeared on the scene and being apprised of the situation offered to take the woman down.

Tash explained carefully what was required. Call in at the police station, he said, and explain that help will be required on the morrow, but that the young man is perfectly safe for the night.

Thus the situation when Ed and I arrived back from our day on the hill. We were naturally full of sympathy for the bloke; did what we could, fed him with Tash's supper, gave him a dram of whisky and even invited him to a game of brag, which he politely declined. Pity, because we were hard up at the time. Still it was all very cosy, with the old pot-boiler stove glowing red and the wind beginning to rise outside the hut.

Little did we know of the drama being played out in Fort Bill: of a distraught wife sobbing out a tale of her husband's desperate plight. She was new to the game, I suppose.

As night progressed the wind rose and with the wind came the rain. It hammered against the thick walls of the hut, roared down the chimney, shook the roof. About midnight I went to pay a reluctant call of nature. It was hell out there, baby . . . most of the Atlantic was being blown horizontally up the valley in great drenching swathes, which is why at first I couldn't believe my eyes . . . surely will o' the wisps don't come out on a night like this, even Scottish ones? A long line of lights was bobbing steadily up the Allt a' Mhuilinn.

I staggered back into the hut with the incredible news.

'The rescue team are coming!'

The young man blanched visibly. 'In this?' he gasped, as the storm rattled the rafters.

We had scarcely put the kettle on before the door burst open and half-a-dozen gigantic Scotsmen, in dripping anoraks, strode into the hut, followed at regular intervals by their mates until the place seemed like a Hogmanay party being held in a phone booth. Coffee all round, and Ed, Tash and I were forced into corners. A little elderly man, who must have been the team mascot or something, was crammed up against me, drinking my coffee. He was obviously enjoying himself. 'Came up here when Linnell was killed, y'know. Nasty business – had his head cut off by the rope.' The others seemed more concerned about the time each had taken from the village, as though it was some sort of masochistic race they were taking part in.

There was at first some doubt as to the victim and the big police sergeant in charge stared hard at Tash, who, I must admit, normally looked like a severe case of exposure and, what with his diet and all, was a pretty grotty sight. But when at last we pointed to the young man with the broken ankle the sergeant turned to him with words of comfort.

'We've come tae rescue you, laddie,' he said.

'But I don't want to be rescued,' the young man stammered, mindful of the Force Ten gale outside.

'We've came tae rescue you, and rescued you're going tae be, laddie!'

So they strapped him on the stretcher and set out into the night and the storm. We went to the door to watch them on their way: the rain lashed down and the burn which they had to cross was a raging torrent. They had some trouble with that burn, I assure you.

'My God, but they're efficient!' said Ed, as we sought the warmth of the hut again. It was a very comforting thing to know, that was.

We never bothered to find out what happened to the young man. Some things are better left as mysteries. My guess is he died of pneumonia.

❊ from *Climber and Rambler* (1975)

L. G. Shadbolt | *Sark Limpets*

As regards the indigenous fauna of Sark, the adhesive limpet takes a prominent place. The more robust specimens may be used as footholds if due warning is given of the coming strain. Lest anyone should be tempted to take out a patent in pocket footholds, let him be warned that it has already been tried. In more youthful and optimistic days I carried out an exhaustive series of experiments with quantities of the largest size in limpets, but, in spite of careful nourishment, they refused to stick to unknown rock faces at the word of command, basely dropping into the sea the moment they were released.

✵ from *Climbers' Club Journal* (1912)

Daloni Seth Hughes | Gully Scramble

One day I thought it would be pleasant to try an unfrequented gully on the Ysgolion Duon. This fine cliff is not a popular haunt – the five miles' trudge, with only a few gully pitches at the end of it, turns most climbers aside – but a view of the great cwm, with its amphitheatre of imposing crags, will repay the walk at any time. I decided to find some way up and invited a couple of friends to come too. One was a slightly built Welshman and the other a definitely heavy-weight German, so we made a rather ill-balanced trio of climbers. However, as we had no rope that didn't matter much.

It was a hot grind up the steep valley path, but we soon cooled down, almost to the point of shivering, when we reached the shadow of the 'Ladders'. We started up a slimy crack, thick with vegetation, and continued over steep, grassy shelves till a definite gully appeared. It seemed to lead right to the top of the cliffs, but unfortunately we were soon scared out of it by an impassable chockstone. Then things began to be slightly uncomfortable. We were forced on to a perpendicular *arête* of unstable rocks, loosely cemented together with wet turf. Presently one of us dislodged a large block, seriously alarming our German friend, whose nose it missed by less than an inch. We longed to regain the safety of our delightful gully, and the only possible way was by a funnel-shaped groove of restricting dimensions. It ended in an easy grass ledge. I wriggled up and the lean man followed. There was a furious scraping of boots, a blond head poked out of the groove, and a dismayed voice inquired: 'Please, what must I do next? I cannot gom up, but I *can* fall down.' Then a more poignant appeal – 'Please, I am slipping, help!' Our courageous second threw himself full length in the mud and tried to fish up the victim. Immediately a muscular arm freed itself from the crack to cling with octopus-like grip round his neck. It was perfectly obvious that it wouldn't be long before he was dragged down, head first, so I had to take a roll in the mud, too, and attach myself firmly to his ankles. There were a few minutes of horrid suspense. Then, snorting and puffing, and accompanied by a loud noise of grating from all the buttons and buckles that foreign people wear about their clothes, the German managed to haul himself out of the hateful groove. He staggered over our prostrate bodies to the furthest corner of the shelf, murmuring 'Tank Gott, I am safe!' and began to devour lettuce sandwiches with silent ferocity. We scrambled up the rest of the gully feeling rather subdued, for we knew quite well that this had not been at all good climbing.

❈ from *Pinnacle Club Journal* (1934)

What the Guidebooks Say

THE GREAT CHIMNEY, CLOGWYN-Y-BUSTACH

H. R. C. Carr

Difficult if none of the pitches are shirked. Most entertaining when done with a large number of large climbers in heavy rain.

Leader needs patience and 40 feet of rope.

Climbing may be begun in the depths of the forest close to the stream, where a grass-covered crag towers above the trees; a cairn at the foot of a mossy wall marks the start. After scaling several minor obstacles, work of a more serious nature is begun 150 feet higher, where it is necessary to penetrate a dense growth of brambles in the direction of an *arête*. A track, useful in descending, is passed *en route*. The rock, when reached, is discovered to be peculiar, but sound. The *arête* leads to a fine natural arch. Swing up to the left and wriggle through a funnel. After a slight descent, move northwards for 60 feet along an easy traverse; primroses bloom here in the spring. Pause at the foot of a black crack, 15 feet high, overshadowed by a birch tree. A convenient bollard and a good hold hidden deep inside the crack are material aids to progress, and when the tree can be grasped, it is as well to resort unashamedly to the habits of a remote ancestry.

On emerging from the upper branches of the tree, one can look in at the window of the Great Chimney, the entrance of which lies a few feet to the right on a commodious terrace. The crack and tree may be avoided by traversing farther to the right and ascending the face for 30 feet to the steep grass below the terrace. This alternative, though easier, is unsatisfactory.

The party now gathers and examines what it has 'come out for to see'. A huge flake has split a few inches from the main mass of the cliff, and has thoughtfully left room in the resulting

fissure for the passage of man. Upon passing the entrance, a glimmer of light will be observed through an exiguous hole high up in the interior of the Chimney. A slim and dainty leader will find little difficulty with the pitch (20 feet), but less adaptable persons will not succeed without 'the windy suspiration of forced breath' in fitting their ampler proportions to the aperture. Having overcome the chockstone, we find ourselves at the bottom of a crypt-like crevasse, lit by a narrower lancet window 40 feet overhead.

These ambitions of a superior virtue may back and knee with great labour directly upwards, but it is more usual to sidle along the floor of the passage which twists, rises and ends 90 feet from the chockstone. Leaving his companions in the cellarage, the leader pulls out of the exit to find himself on a pleasant ledge beside a large belay. Nothing remains except 30 feet of easy climbing to the grass ledges at the top of the crag.

A quick line of descent will be found about 50 yards away in the direction of Llyn Gwynant down a grassy opening in the cliff.

It may be of some use to mention that the rope is useless inside the chimney and a man is quite likely to become hopelessly jammed if those above him try to haul him up. At certain seasons, too, it is as well to remember that the climb *and* the descent from it are considerably harder and more painful when done in the dark.

Many variations have been worked out on this climb; some of them lead to nowhere: the route and its mistakes are well scratched. An outside finish, which avoids the main point of the climb, is possible. It is steep and exposed. It is not described for the climb *is* the Chimney.

❁ from A Climber's Guide to Snowdon (1926)

AVALANCHE ROUTE, LLIWEDD

J. M. Archer Thomas and A. W. Andrews

The most exposed climb in England and Wales. Exceedingly difficult but delectable in good weather, indefensible in bad. Best number, two. Ninety feet of rope required. Good balance essential. No aid and little protection can be given to the leader. Only for a thoroughly expert party. Steepness. Absence of grass and gravel. Excellence of rock. Exiguity of holds. Long distance between belays. A succession of breezy situations.

RED WALL CONTINUATION. More exposed than wall of Devil's Kitchen, but safer in so far as the rock is perfectly sound. Ninety-foot interval. Leader ascends 70 to 80 feet alone. No prodigious feats of strength, but constant muscular tension. One fancy foothold of limited utility. An operation of exceptional delicacy.

❁ from Climbs on Lliwedd (1909)

INTERMEDIATE GULLY, DOW CRAG

George S. Bower

Severe; strenuous; 80-foot rope.

There are members of the Club to whom 'Intermediate' is more than a climb; rather is its ascent one of the solemn rites connected with the practice of a cult. To one such disciple did I write, asking for a description of the preparations necessary on the part of those who would attain to this *cercle*. The reply came by wire: 'Train on Raw meat and Stout, use Bulldog buttons . . .' In the framing of the following notes, it has been assumed that the would-be climber is suitably prepared . . .

❀ from *Doe Crags and Climbs Around Coniston* (1922)

THE IDWAL SLABS

J. M. Edwards

The climbing is much of the stepping-up type . . .

The characters of continuous delicacy are illustrated by the fact that the Slabs were not exploited until 1915 and by the link of their history with such a climber as I. A. Richards. Nowadays they are not so select, and scratches both short and long cover the face with the studious abandon of the times. It is perhaps well that rubbers are more discreet. First and last the Slabs are a matter of Faith, Hope and Charity.

❀ from *Cwm Ideal Group* (1936)

ON TRYFAN

J. M. Edwards

The whole buttress is really much broken up, but with a little looking and care the climb is amusing enough. Nor is its character impossibly light. With ingenuity one might well get stuck on it, for instance; and so the climb is well worth while. The route described is a picked one, from many. (Nor' Nor' Buttress)

The climbing is varied and energetic, less frequently the exactly expected than on most Tryfan routes. A simple grabbing technique does answer, but the route has charm of position and some exposure and continuity of interest. (Gashed Crag)

It is a climb that retains its interest and its difficulty over all its distance. It has not all the delicacy of Long Chimney, but has character of its own. In difficulty, one moves each time after the fashion of a crab. The general layout of it is challenging. As is the habit of Tryfan the holds that should arrive, arrive well. (Scars Climb)

❊ from *Tryfan Group* (1937)

GRASSY GULLY, PONTESFORD ROCKS

W. Unsworth

The gully which divides the two main buttresses has enjoyed various names from time to time, not all of them polite. This guide book returns to the name originally bestowed on the gully by the pioneers, thus demonstrating that history is more powerful than mere emotion.

❊ from *A Climber's Guide to Pontesford Rocks* (1962)

WHITE SCAR

Dave Knighton and Al Phizacklea

Known locally as 'Indian Country', this blatantly extrovert crag dominates the scene from the A590 two and a half miles W of Levens Bridge. It is a large limestone crag which is situated at the southern end of the Whitbarrow escarpment.

This crag is probably the most difficult inland crag to get to in England. At its base is a horrendously steep section of quarried scree 150 feet high, and at its top is steep grass separated by several tiers of shattered rock. The atmosphere is more akin to a sea cliff than an inland crag . . .

Routes (1) to (3) are generally reached by abseil, but care is needed because the rope can easily dislodge loose blocks above the crag itself, and for the same reason helmets may be regarded as being essential. Retreats from any of these routes would be problematic to say the least, and so it is wise to leave abseil ropes in place. The base of the crag is also festooned with man-eating brambles, to add extra spice. The routes on Space Buttress are more easily accessible with good belays and with care an escape can be made along the base of the crag to the R.

It is only fair to warn that many routes have not yet been repeated.

White Scar is a crag with an acquired taste; once the initial fears are overcome, it is a most exciting place to climb.

❀ from *Rock Climbs, Lancashire and the North West* (1983)

Showell | # The Ballad
Styles | # of Idwal Slabs

EDITOR'S INTRODUCTION The climbing world of thirty years ago seems a very innocent place viewed in retrospect. The days of Wall End Barn or Scotty Dwyer's annexe, when climbing, boozing and *laughing* all seemed part of the same game, seem a million miles away from our competitive modern scene. Most of our songs then were culled from rugby clubs and therefore by definition dirty – but we did have our own 'poem': a doggerel verse by Showell Styles. It was recited and even *acted* at club dinners. I mean of course *The Ballad of Idwal Slabs*.

It was published in *The Mountaineer's Week-End Book*, but that has been out of print for many years now – a pity, because the Ballad forms a distinctive footnote in our climbing heritage and shouldn't be lost. Others evidently feel the same, for it was revived at a couple of dinners this year, so I make no excuse for reprinting it here.

I asked Pip Styles how it came about, and this is what he says:

'1947. Hemp climbing-ropes, clinkers and tricounis, crampons a bit of a snigger and *piton* a dirty word. Christmas at Glan Dena, the M.A.M.'s North Wales hut. Plucking and drawing of the Christmas Dinner goose achieved with the aid of two medical students who insisted on dissecting its ear. Ears, eyes and nose full of goose-down, muscles comfortably slack after leading Zigzag and Home Climb on Gribin Facet. Voice from kitchen: "What about something to get the fun started after the Dinner?" Ejected goose-down, collected pencil and paper, invoked the Muse of Doggerel and wrote the Ballad at a sitting.'

THE BALLAD OF IDWAL SLABS
(To be spoken dramatically in costume:
deerstalker hat, side-whiskers, and alpenstock)

I'll tell you the tale of a climber; a drama of love on the crags;
A story to pluck at your heart-strings, and tear your emotions
        to rags.
He was tall, he was fair, he was handsome; John Christopher
        Brown was his name;
The Very Severes nearly bored him to tears – and he felt about
        girls much the same.

Till one day, while climbing at Ogwen, he fell (just a figure of
        speech)
For the President's beautiful daughter, named Mary Jane
        Smith – what a peach!
Her figure was slim as Napes Needle, her lips were as red as
        Red Wall;
A regular tiger, she's been up the Eiger North Wall, with no
        pitons at all!

Now Mary had several suitors, but never a one would she take,
Though it seemed that she favoured one fellow, a villain
        named Reginald Hake;
This Hake was a Cad who used pitons, and wore a long silken
        moustarsh,
Which he used, so they say, as an extra belay – but perhaps we
        are being too harsh.

John took Mary climbing on Lliwedd, and proposed while on
        Mallory's Slab;
It took him three pitches to do it, for he hadn't much gift of the
        gab.
He said: 'Just belay for a moment – there's a little spike close to
        your knee –
And tell me, fair maid, when you're properly belayed, would
        you care to hitch up with me?'

Said Mary, 'It's only a toss-up between you and Reginald
        Hake.
And the man I am going to marry must perform some great
        deed for my sake.

I will marry whichever bold climber shall excel at the following
      feat –
To climb headfirst down Hope, with no rubbers or rope,
At our very next climbing-club Meet!'

Now when Mary told the Committee, she had little occasion to
      plead,
For she was as fair as a jug-handle hold at the top of a
      hundred-foot lead.
The Club ratified her proposal, and the President had to agree;
He was fond of his daughter, but felt that she oughter
Get married, between you and me.

           *   *   *   *   *

There was quite a big crowd for the contest, lined up at the
      foot of the Slabs;
The Mobs came from Bangor in Buses, and the Nobs came
      from Capel in Cabs.
There were Fell and Rock, Climbers', and Rucksack, and the
      Pinnacle Club (in new hats)
And – sight to remember! – an Alpine Club Member, in very
      large crampons and spats!

The weather was fine for a wonder; the rocks were as dry as a
      bone.
Hake arrived with a crowd of his backers, but John Brown
      strode up quite alone;
A rousing cheer greeted the rivals; a coin was produced, and
      they tossed.
'Have I won?' cried John Brown as the penny came down.
'No, you fool!' hissed his rival. 'You've lost!'

So Hake had first go at the contest; he went up by the
      Ordinary Route,
And only the closest observer would have noticed a bulge in
      each boot.
Head first he came down the top pitches, applying his
      moustache as brake;
He didn't relax till he'd passed the Twin Cracks, and the crowd
      shouted, 'Attaboy, Hake!'

At the foot of the Slabs Hake stood sneering, and draining a
    bottle of Scotch;
'Your time was ten seconds,' the President said, consulting the
    Treasurer's watch.
'Now, Brown, if you'd win, you must beat that.' Our hero's
    sang froid was sublime;
He took one look at Mary, and – light as a fairy – ran up to the
    top of the climb.

Now though Hake had made such good going, John wasn't
    discouraged a bit,
For that he was the speedier climber even Hake would have
    had to admit.
So, smiling as though for a snapshot, not a hair of his head out
    of place,
Our hero John Brown started wriggling down – but look! what
    a change on his face!

Prepare for a shock, gentle ladies; gentle*men*, check the
    blasphemous word;
For the villainy I am to speak of is such as you never have
    heard!
Reg Hake had cut holes in the toes of his boots, and filled up
    each boot with soft soap!
As he slid down the climb, he had covered with slime every handhold
    and foothold on Hope!

Conceive (if you can) the tense horror that gripped the vast
    concourse below,
When they saw Mary's lover slip downwards like an arrow
    that's shot from a bow!
'He's done for!' gasped twenty score voices. 'Stand from
    under!' roared John from above.
As he shot down the slope, he was steering down Hope – still
    fighting for life and for love!

Like lightning he flew past the Traverse – in a flash he had
    reached the Twin Cracks –
The friction was something terrific – there was smoke coming
    out of his slacks –

He bounced on the shelf at the top of Pitch Two, and bounded
    clean over its edge!
A shout of 'He's gone!' came from all – except one; and that
    one, of course, was our Reg.

But it's not the expected that happens – in this sort of story, at
    least;
And just as John thought he was finished, he found that his
    motion had ceased!
His braces (pre-war and elastic) had caught on a small rocky
    knob,
And so, safe and sound, he came gently to ground 'mid the
    deafening cheers of the mob!

'Your time was *five* seconds!' the President cried. 'She's yours,
    my boy – take her! You win!'
'My hero!' breathed Mary, and kissed him, while Hake gulped
    a bottle of gin,
And tugged his moustache as he whispered, 'Aha! my
    advances you spurn!
Curse a chap that wins races by using his braces!' and he slunk
    away, ne'er to return.

They were wed at the Church of St Gabbro, and the Vicar,
    quite carried away,
Did a hand-traverse into his pulpit, and shouted out 'Let us
    belay!'
John put the ring on Mary's finger – a snap-link it was, made
    of steel,
And they walked to the taxis 'neath an arch of ice-axes, while
    all the bells started to peal.
The Morals we draw from this story are several, I'm happy to
    say;
It's Virtue that wins in the long run; long silken moustaches
    don't pay;
Keep the head uppermost when you're climbing; if you *must*
    slither, be on a rope;
Steer clear of the places that sell you cheap braces – and the
    fellow that uses Soft Soap!

❀ from *The Mountaineer's Week-End Book* (1950)

II. Playing Away

John Barry | It's an Ill Wind

Half of Italy, it seemed, was parked in the Val Ferret that same day. And not your orderly British parking either, but real hot-blooded Latin stuff with modest family saloons serving in the office of Grand Prix thoroughbreds four-wheel-drifting into the happy spaghetti chaos. Panache, perhaps, was the word for it. We parked: sans panache, nicely off the road and decently square to at least one of the surrounding Regazzonis. Smug was the word for it.

Then it was off up the path toward the Triolet hut and the second ascent of the Gogna/Rata route on the North Face of the Aiguille de Leschaux – at least that was the plan as confidently pronounced by the apprentice.

For a hut walk this one was a pleasant plod – 'doddle' was the word for it – and since it was a Sunday the way lay dotted with shapely and occasionally entwined diversions. Davey Nicholls Sebastian Coe'd it as usual while I made my token attempt to keep up until heart, lungs and legs mutinied – successfully, whereafter I fell, wonderfully diverted, to the rear.

Arriving at the hut some hours later, I found Davey engaging a Lorenesque Italian in a one-sided conversation based on home-brewed esperanto. She was a stotter wearing shorts of Whillans brevity, legs 3 pitches long and 5C all the way and Dad suspicious of Davey's intentions – and rightly so. Unfortunately for my partner, she'd never heard of Gogna or Rata so he scored no points at all with his North-Face namedropping, and, sadly soon tiring of Davey's chorus, she flounced gorgeously away leaving him to Signeurs Gogna, Rata and me. 'Musta lost something in the translation,' said our Lothario hopefully.

Next day the weather was shaky – very warm and cloudy – but we decided to have a 'look' all the same. Half-way up the initial ice slope, adjudged fifty degrees in the guide, but happily little over forty degrees, we called it a day. Water was running everywhere and we backed off at the thought of what the conditions would be like on the much more serious top two-thirds of the route. 'What do you think, mate?' – that time-honoured euphemism for 'Let's push off, this is ridiculous'. It takes the braver or saner man to deploy either version, for it force-feeds the other's ego and affords him a distinct tactical advantage. I agreed absolutely but said 'Could give it a couple more pitches' . . . My heart sank as he agreed – then a couple of bouncing bricks said don't be daft and down we went.

From the glacier as dawn broke we looked back at the face to get a close-up of the line for future forays. Our gaze was drawn leftwards to a couloir which ran out of the top left corner of the initial ice field. It led uninterrupted to the summit ridge, steepening in the last third to a near-vertical seam of ice. Well, they're all near-vertical, aren't they? It was an open invitation to anyone who has traded punches with Scottish ice, or wildly flailed a shorty axe in a wet Welsh winter and dulled a dozen crampon points in between. A new route? There was no mention

'Legs was much impressed.'

of it in our guide or in the Vallot. 'Give it a try next time up?' 'OK.' And so, faint failure soothed by half-hearted hope and fuelled on procrastinating dreams, we retreated to the hut and a brew. A gallon or so of tea later we decided that two axes apiece and perhaps some ice screws would be handy – not to mention some liquid courage – so it was back to the valley.

Half-way down a patch of snow that interrupted the hut path we overtook Legs Loren tripping delicately and deliciously downward. This was the signal for Nicholls, who'll stoop to anything for a friendly smile or more, and who in winter masquerades as a ski-instructor of sorts, to burst into a tight-legged, short swinging glissade that would not have disgraced Stenmark. Legs was much impressed as our hero jet-turned neatly round a rock and paralleled casually to a stop at the bottom. In a vain attempt to follow, I fell heavily at the first gate and gashed my forearm on the pick of an axe that was too carelessly attached to my sac. Salvaging what dignity I could, I limped down clutching the wound with the other hand in an attempt to conceal the damage. But blood dripped on to the snow and with it my morale and machismo. Nicholls, with ever an eye for the main chance, gained more points by bandaging my arm and rather too literally adding insult to injury. With a triumphant wave to Legs he bounded off toward the road with a whole new enthusiasm.

'Troubles always come in threes,' said Davey sagely as we neared the road. 'Probably find your car has been nicked. Should round your day off nicely,' he added cheerfully. Rounding a corner, we came upon the car, now parked in splendid isolation, just in time to see it being towed on to the back of a breakdown truck – Italian style. Now you might imagine that the nation that created Ferrari, Maserati, Lamborghini *et al.* would be car lovers and you'd be wrong – unless it was just that this particular BL vintage was beneath their contempt.

For whatever reason, a winch-cable had been attached to a distinctly sub-standard belay and before a panic-stricken sprint brought me within distance, my wheels were hauled unceremoniously on to the back of the truck. Off came bumper and silencer and down went four tyres.

I know my Italians (but sadly no Italian). They are an

unreasonable and wildly excitable race and a bit of British calm would soon sort this out.

'What the bloody hell d'you think you are doing with my car?' I howled, gesticulating in a most Italian way in the not entirely mistaken belief that this would translate English into passable Italian. From somewhere beneath a hugely sad groucho moustache the Carabiniere who was supervising the growing shambles replied 'calmo, calmo', very calmly, very reasonably and in a thoroughly Northern European sort of way. Something seemed to have gone wrong. The only word of Italian I knew was 'grazzi', which wasn't quite the word I wanted just then. 'Parlez-vous français?' I asked without being too clear as to how I would proceed if his answer was 'Oui', since my schoolboy variety is fine for pens, aunts, charabangs and postilions but not so hot on the infinitely more useful phrases such as 'Get my bloody car off the back of that bloody lorry', etc. etc. Il simply no comprende, and despite my reversion to English reinforced by animated semaphore, we remained incommunicado.

The breakdown truck took off all but literally, with my car perched precariously atop and siren wailing and all lights flashing – somewhat unnecessarily, since apart from the 'persona dramatis', the place was deserted for miles. It two-wheeled into the first hairpin and Regazzonied into the blue.

We set off in hot, steaming hot, pursuit, doubting whether we'd ever see our car again, but hours later, having tracked smouldering rubber and sundry BL accessories to a third-rate garage in down-town Courmayeur, we traced my offending wheels. The necessary repairs had been carefully botched and release was eventually secured at a mere umpteen thousand lire.

'Just one of those days,' said Davey helpfully. That night, beer-cheered, I consoled myself that at least he might have forgotten about his new line. So you'll forgive my lack of enthusiasm when the very next day my partner announced that we were going to have another go. Confident that sanity would ultimately prevail, I allowed him to indulge himself in a bit of gear-sorting. I pointed out that between us we had six pegs, four of which were identical and very senior knife blades – and had not Gogna used seventy on a route not a couple of rope's lengths away? This deterred him not at all, and knowing my man

I gave up and buckled to. We decided against bivvy gear – more than a stove, that is. Dave's theory was that since the route was mainly ice we wouldn't be slowed by technical intricacies and what wouldn't fall to stealth could be reduced by 'piolet à bludgeon' in a frontal assault.

And so it was that we found ourselves crossing the same glacier the day after at two in the morning. By three we were at the top of the ice slope and preparing to sally on to new ground. The way ahead was uncertain and fairly steep, so we decided to await the comforting and hopefully revealing light of dawn. A brew helped to while away the time and t o up morale. At last the dawn dayed fine and, spotting a line, we climbed on.

It was great. Exciting as new ground always is; but more than that the climbing was superb, the protection passable and the belays not half bad. It was warm too. A bit too warm really, but at least the ice was soft and sensuously rubbery – if you like that sort of thing. On we went searching, seeking, sensing the way if you were leading and with one eye on the pitch after if you were holding the rope.

For the most part the ice gave the line so we followed our noses and they rarely lied, and though the ground steepened it was still all very reasonable. We were happy in our work and chatted cheerfully whenever we met. I led a pitch, drove in a peg and belayed. Dave came up, at the gallop, took some gear and led on. 'OK, mate,' he yelled, meaning that he was belayed. I untied from my peg and began to knock it out when a steady roar caught my mind's ear. Leaving the peg I glanced around the cirque in the hope of a glimpse of something spectacular. Nothing doing. Returning to the peg I became aware of a darkening above. A quick look up. Shit! Dave had already seen it and was road-runner flat against the hill. The vision was quick, the impression quicker and the memory hazy, but I recall huge blocks of ice and seemingly endless cascades of slow snow streaming off the summit slopes and out, out, out into the sky above us. Escape looked unlikely and, too frightened to panic, we cravenly cowered – and survived. Ice broke on rocks all about, but none on us, while snow buffeted but left us attached until at last the sky cleared and the discovery that I was unscathed encouraged me to inquire after Davey. 'Dave, Dave, you O K?' No answer. Panic. How to get down, rescue, insurance, me, me, me?

'I'm O K, what will we do?' – a small voice miles off at 150 feet away. 'It's this bloody couloir.'

'Same up or down – and we're nearer the top,' I answered with half-hearted, half-convinced reason.

There being nothing more to say the rope went tight, I removed the peg and went on up to Dave. Together we were braver – though still very shaken. But it would be safer ahead, steeper and therefore safer, and in any case there was probably no more to come – we argued with a logic short on alternatives.

In other circumstances the remaining 800 feet would have been exhilarating, but the joy had been swept away and we had even stopped pretending. At the time survival seemed a serious business, only regaining its sense of humour in the retelling. As the pitches got wilder, the belays precarious and the protection mere pretence our banter evaporated altogether. The joke had been overworked.

The penultimate pitch was a crippler. Six feet of the couloir had fallen away at its narrowest point, leaving smooth crampon-resistant rock beneath. A long reach failed by miles and a full tiptoeing stretch by inches. A peg for help, some wild piolet à panic, a couple of what your modern cragrat describes as 'armlocks' and enough height gained to get the front point, alarmingly close to the bottom of the ice, on to the continuation of the couloir. A few feet later I belayed with all four remaining pegs. 'Short pitch that,' observed Dave.

The last pitch was a beauty – virgin white ice leading at eighty degrees up to the sun and what appeared to be easy ground. I led on. Oh boy, beautiful ice. Steep but compliantly axe-worthy, though a touch too soft for screws and a long way to anywhere. The exposure was sobering. 'Relax, man, relax,' I coaxed myself aloud. But if the ice stays you can't fail with modern tools, can you? It stayed and so did I – all the way up 150 feet to a belay boulder that Michelangelo himself couldn't have improved on. I gave a wild scraich of unabashed joy. No need for coy smugness here; whooped our pleasure at being out of it. Chuffed was the word.

Climbing was fun again and promises of future prudence

made privately lower down were well on their way to being forgotten, as was the avalanche, though that would assuredly be resurrected, elaborated and adorned in a dozen versions and a hundred beers from now. After all, why let accuracy stand in the way of a good story?

We sat in the sun and admired a fantastic view of the North side of the Jorasses. 'At least ED "Sup",' pronounced Dave authoritatively. 'No doubt about it,' I replied without having the slightest idea what ED Sup actually meant. A wet of tea later we had moderated to ED Inf, and later still, recovering our sense of proportion and fearing ridicule, TD Sup seemed to be popular. I still have no idea what grade it really was – and what does it matter, for doubtless in but a short while some callow youth will have reduced it to a 2-hour Difficile – and mayhap Legs Loren will show it to be an easy day for oh what a lady. And good luck to them: the only advice I'd presume to offer is 'Mind where you park your car, mate'!

❦ from *Climber and Rambler* (1982)

H. W. Tilman | Eating on Everest, 1938

I must confess I was surprised to hear any criticism of the food, except from Odell, who has not yet finished criticizing the food we ate on Nanda Devi in 1936 and who, in spite of his semi-starved condition, succeeded in getting to the top.

I am sure that Dr Warren as well as Dr Raymond Greene will be interested to hear that we consulted a dietician in 1935, and though Raymond Greene was not there Warren was, and he will bear me out that the food we then had was much more Spartan than that which we had on the 1938 Everest expedition. As you know, dietitians have little sympathy with human nature. No two people agree about food, not even husband and wife. But the whole art of travel is to adapt oneself to circumstances. The Everest expedition involves more travelling than actual climbing and, as you have already heard, the difficulty on the mountain is that one does not want to eat any food whatever. In the opinion of at least two of those on the mountain we lived like Sybarites, but I am aware that there are degrees of sybaritism, if one may use the word. Up at Camp 3 we certainly lived very well; above that the choice of food is not particularly vital because of the fact that one does not want to eat at all.

I have already told you what we had to eat, and we found at Rongbuk at least forty boxes of 1936 stores, which some of the party were pleased to see. They contained nutritious things like pickles and liver extracts. I remember as we were about to leave Gangtok the Maharajah gave us a farewell dinner, and very excellent it was. Noticing how wistfully my comrades were regarding the last course of the five-course dinner and having to make a speech in reply to the Maharajah, I suggested that they had all the appearance of men who had undergone a long fast, or were about to undergo one. And I ventured to remind them of a saying by Thoreau, the great apostle of the simple life who lived alone in the American woods and wrote a book about

it, that most of the luxuries and nearly all the so-called comforts
of life are not only not indispensable but positively a hindrance
to the elevation of mankind.

❄ from *Mount Everest, 1938* (1948)

Robert Schultheis | Khyber Taxi

There we were, Peter and I, at the Afghan–Pakistan border at the foot of the Khyber Pass . . . Peter was an Australian who had been working as a bartender in Earl's Court, London, and was wending his way slowly home via the Overland route through Europe and Asia; I was on my way back to Nepal for a season of trekking and climbing.

We could have picked up a bus there at the border – the rickety-but-reliable Pakistani bus, or the equally rickety but equally reliable Afghan mail bus – either one of them would have transported us, for a few rupees, safely over the Khyber to Peshawar.

We could probably also have hitched with one of the 'hip' overland tour buses that were stopped at the border – Rainbow, or Magic Bus . . . or even the posh Rötel German Tour Bus, with its waiters serving Bratwurst and Löwenbrau to the Deutschlanders aboard – two clever lads like ourselves should have been able to con our way into a free ride between the border and Peshawar with a good hard-luck story . . .

But no: it was the Khyber Taxi for us. 'It'll be a lark,' Peter said cheerily, twisting his mustache and grinning with the optimism of the completely ignorant. (Whenever an Australian says something is going to be 'a lark', watch out for flying objects. I had already experienced a couple of Peter's 'larks' earlier in the trip – including a visit to the roughest bar-and-brothel in eastern Turkey – and each time we had been lucky to get away with a whole hide and wallets intact.)

'Only way to see the country,' I agreed sententiously, 'or get away from the tourist crowd and mingle with the people.'

That the people we proposed to mingle with were the most notorious cut-throats and brigands of Central Asia did not seem to make an impression on us at the time.

At any rate, we strolled out of the Pakistani customs shed on that hot, sunny morning, and immediately someone hissed at us – 'Ssssst!' – and stepped out from the shadows where he had been lurking.

Before us appeared a wondrous and terrible figure of a man. He stood fully six-feet-four-inches tall, sported a full beard and long hair streaked ash-blond and rust-red with henna; wore a turban; and was wrapped in what appeared to be a filthy striped bedsheet, under which was visible a pair of decrepit grey pajamas and size-fourteen basketball shoes. My stare ended with the red fingernail polish on the nails of his enormous, filthy hands and, on his right wrist, a watch with no dial.

This apparition grinned encouragingly at us, and gave us the traditional greeting of the East: '*You want to change money?*'

'No.'

We made to walk past him but he moved into our path like a crab, still smiling. 'Buy hasheesh?'

'No.'

'Opium?'

'No.'

'Heroeen?'

'No.'

He thought for a moment, grimacing up his huge face. 'El es dee?'

'No.'

Again a moment of painful cogitation – then his face lit up again.

'Passport? Franchy? Eyetalian?'

'*No.*'

'Gold? Sell in India, make good money?'

Now, *that* was a good scam – smuggling gold into India is one of the last great rackets an amateur can get into with a reasonable hope of success. Like the Changmai Opium Caper, or the illegal importation of Cadillacs into Iran, it was a good bet. But, alas, we had no money to invest in a Khyber-to-Bombay bullion run.

'No,' we said, sadly.

'*Gun?* Any kind gun? Pistol, machine gun, A-R?'

'No thanks.'

The Pathan looked quite downcast, like a magician who has pulled his last rabbit out of the hat and has not heard a single clap of applause.

'He . . . brought us face to face with what was evidently the driver . . .'

'But,' Peter spoke up suddenly, 'we *do* need a taxi to Peshawar!'

'AH!' Immediately the disgruntled giant was transfigured into action – a *deal*! The joy supreme, the life's blood of any Central Asian! In an instant he was dragging us by the arms, our packs slung over his shoulders, bellowing ahead in Pashto to a crowd of about twenty ne'er-do-wells milling around a 1951 Chevrolet parked a way up the dusty street. He elbowed a path through the mob for us and brought us face to face with what was evidently the driver – a shorter, sly-looking Pathan in torn, shiny green pants, slippers, a Grand Funk Railroad T-shirt and a skull cap. A breakneck dialogue in Pashto followed, for about twenty seconds. Then our mentor turned to us and said, with an admirably straight face: 'He take you Peshawar taxi two hundred rupees each.'

Now, two hundred Pakistani rupees is about twenty dollars – totally out of the question for the few hours across the Khyber.

'Oh, no, he won't,' Peter exclaimed, never at a loss for words in such situations. 'He is *crazy* man . . . criminal . . .' (By leaving out articles and prepositions, he thought he could make himself more easily understood.) 'He is *bad* man . . . lunatic . . .'

The big Pathan looked at me questioningly.

'Too much, too much,' I said. And to add weight to our bargaining we reshouldered our packs and began to walk away. That set off a great spasm of shouting, and the giant ran around in front of us, holding up his hands, wailing piteously: 'Wait! Wait! No go!'

We stopped, and then everybody jabbered in Pashto for about ten more seconds before the giant turned to us again. 'O K – how much you pay?'

'Two rupees each,' I said, neatly slicing the fare by one thousand per cent. There was a howl of outrage from the driver, the giant put a fluttering hand to his heart – like an elderly maiden about to swoon – and a deafening cacophony broke out among the crowd, the confusion abetted by a tiny, English-speaking Pakistani's interpolations: 'This chap is saying he needs more money to buy petrol – I have heard Western women are not wearing underpants – this chap needs oil for taxi or it will not go . . .'

Finally, we settled on the princely sum of four rupees (about forty cents) apiece, plus a rupee apiece to the bearded giant for his role in arranging the deal. He shook our hands till the bones cracked, then went off chuckling, crinkling his two rupee notes, to buy a cup of chai and some rice and kebab at the dingy café across the road.

Peter and I crammed into the front seat of the taxi, along with our packs, the driver and the little English-speaking Paki; four Pathans jammed into the back seat – two of them with antique muzzle-loaders, one with an old Enfield and the fourth with a great burlap sack of pink rubber boots he had bought or stolen somewhere.

'These other rag-bags must be waiting for another taxi,' Peter said, indicating the rest of the crowd still milling around the cab. But no. The remaining dozen-or-so Pathans clambered on to the hood, the roof and into the luggage compartment of the car, and with a great blasting of the horn and gunning of the engine, we lurched into gear and headed east out of Torkham-Khyber, heading toward those dusty, desolate mountains, the gateway of Muslim invaders moving down into India to imperialize and plunder . . . that ancient bandit country, where so many famous people have for so long fought and died: Cary Grant and Errol Flynn and Victor McLaughlin . . . ten thousand cinematic soldiers, marching from the east, up into the Khyber, bagpipes playing, flags waving . . . while the wily Pathans, led by Basil Rathbone, lie in ambush among the rocks . . .

As a path of invasion, the Khyber has almost always led one way – toward the east. The Hindus never managed to spread their amorphous, messy empires westward on to the Central Asian Altiplano, and the British were annihilated when they tried to extend the Raj up through the Khyber into Afghanistan. No, the Khyber leads east, always; and always the Pathans watch, and wait, from the surrounding mountains. They've waited for centuries for trading caravans, or defeated armies, or unsuspecting expeditionary forces – waited, and then picked them to pieces.

And it is still so. The Pakistani Government has little real control over the region, maintaining only a vague suzerainty over the area west of the Indus. And the Pathans go on raiding and smuggling and fighting one another and anyone else who comes along and dreaming of an independent country of their own, to be called 'Pushtunistan'. It would be an odd country, to be sure – something like a one-hundred-by-two-hundred-mile wasteland of waterless mountains, populated by Medieval Muslim Hell's Angels . . .

The rough road climbed steeply through stony escarpments – famished, sun-beaten hills; past abandoned fortifications, and the walled adobe villages of the Pathans, with their Islamic banners waving, and narrow gun-slits along the tops of the high walls. An occasional spot of faded jade green marred the grey sameness of the land, indicating a well or a spring – but there were few of those.

The old Chevy coughed and sputtered; clouds of dust poured in through the windows. The Pathans on the hood and on the roof leaned down to goggle at the *'ferranjee'*, the foreign devils. This irritated Peter, who shook his fist and made absurd faces at our inquisitive fellow travelers. His actions, of course, had the effect of amusing and entertaining the innocent fellows, who thought it was a show being put on for their benefit – soon there were half-a-dozen faces glued to the outside of the windshield, grinning and gaping, reducing the driver's field of view to almost nothing. I shrugged fatalistically and lit up a K-2, one of those execrable Pakistani cigarettes, and puffed away. Peter sighed and managed to gulp a Mandrax tablet down his parched throat.

The driver looked over at my cigarette.

'Chunts?' he asked.

'Chunts? What's a bloody "Chunt"?'

'*Chent*,' said the English-speaking Pakistani. 'Chent cigarettes. American cigarettes, very good, very fine esmoking.'

'Oh, *Kents*. No, no Kents.'

'No Chunts,' the driver said, and shook his head gloomily.

Suddenly, without warning, there was a geyser of steam from the front of the car, and a yell from one of the passengers on the hood as he tumbled off (luckily, we were only going about ten kilometers an hour on the steep grade). We swerved off the road and ground to a halt.

'Wonderful,' said Peter sarcastically. 'Marvelous. How far have we come, five kilometers?'

'Not far,' I said.

Everyone disembarked and the driver trudged off down the road with a jerry can to get water for the radiator.

'Radiator broken,' said the little Pakistani sagaciously.

'Really?' Peter said, as if amazed. 'You must be a master mechanic, eh?'

'No,' chirped the Paki. 'I am advocate – civil – how you say it?'

'Lawyer? Attorney?' I suggested.

'Yes, yes, Attorney-at-Law!'

'*Jailbird*-at-law, more likely,' Peter whispered to me. He was chewing up another Mandrax tablet, always a bad sign – after two or three of them he became a stumbling idiot, useless in emergencies.

'Yes, I am important attorney in Rawalpindi,' the little fellow went on proudly. 'I am sitting on District Magistrate. I have house, car and bicycle. You must come stay with me. You are having paper and pen?'

'Good Lord,' Peter moaned loudly, as I handed the supposed attorney a Nabisco biscuit wrapper and a ballpoint pen. The Paki wrote carefully, painstakingly, for a long, long time, leaning on the hood of the car. Finally he handed the paper back and we read:

> ANWER SAYED
> Forsythganj Cantonment
> Rawalpindi, PAKISTAN
> Attorney-at-Law
> Suites and Tortes.

'Sounds like a bloody baker – "suites and tortes",' Peter snorted.

'You can come with me, we will have jolly time,' Anwer piped.

'Yes, that would be nice,' I said, trying to sound sincere (hospitality from the middle-class Asian is rarely without ulterior motives – the Western guest is a turkey, to be plucked for everything possible).

'Yeah, *nice*,' Peter muttered cynically. 'Wake up in the middle of the night and find him and his six cousins in bed with you, more than likely.'

Australian men are positively *obsessed* with homosexuals, whom they refer to derogatorily as 'poofters'. Muslim culture includes a tradition of strong, rather passionate male bonding, which often becomes sexual in expression – young men flirt, hold hands, carry on affairs . . . It is actually quite charming, once you get used to being around it, but not at all charming to the super-*macho*, primitive Aussies, who regard anything less than chest-thumping masculinity as unthinkable, horrifying.

'If you keep gobbling those mandies, you'll be out cold before we reach Peshawar. I'll rent you out at ten rupees a go to the Pathans,' I said unkindly.

'Aw, have a heart, mate. Make it at least twenty. Think of me poor ass.'

Eventually, the radiator was filled and 'patched'. We all piled into and on to the car again, and off we went.

'And about time, too,' as Peter rightly said. The afternoon was getting on, and the Khyber Pass is no place for two *ferranjees*, sahibs or infidels to be caught out after dark. In fact, there is a sign on the road over the Khyber, put up by the Pakistani Government, to that effect:

KHYBER PASS
Tribal Area – Danger
Travel Prohibited After Dark

At this rate we would still be on the pass at sunset, somewhere out in the Doom Country between Landi Kotal and Peshawar; then the knives would come out, and the guns, and two more unbelieving dogs would join the long roll of the victims of the Khyber.

'Well, here's Landi Kotal, anyway,' Peter said grudgingly a few minutes later, as the overloaded cab coughed and wheezed into the potholed main street of that infamous town, center of smuggling, gun manufacturing and tribal warfare.

It was a grim-looking place, like the Dodge City or Tombstone of our American myths – only this was real, all too real. Every other man on the street was armed to the teeth. There were groups of men on every corner, eyeing each other suspiciously. One really savage-looking gent sported a machine pistol and *two* M-16s with banana clips. He looked over at the taxi, saw us, frowned fearfully and spat on the sidewalk.

A moment later, to our dismay, the taxi pulled over to the curb and stopped. 'CHAI!' the driver bellowed. There were coos and cries of delight from the Pathans as they unloaded.

'Oh, no!' cried Peter.

'Yes, yes, he is stopping for a spot of tea and luncheon,' our little friend said.

'But we haven't gone ten miles. This is ridiculous!' Peter said several unprintable words, including a suggestion that the entire Khyber Pass commit an anatomical impossibility upon itself.

'Yes, yes, with biscuits too,' the uncomprehending Anwer agreed enthusiastically.

We all squeezed out of the car and crowded through a literal hole in the wall into a dim mud room that reeked like ethyl mercaptan. A crowd of Pathans was jammed around wooden tables, shovelling down appalling-looking servings of rice and curry and sucking up cups of muddy milk tea, while Paki film music roared from a radio in the corner. It seemed a fair approximation of Hell, one of Breughelian fiendishness.

The 'luncheon' could not be said to have been a great success. For one thing, Peter and I were famished, not having eaten since dinner the night before in Kabul, and so we made the mistake of ordering the Landi Kotal *plat du jour*.

It was, to put it mildly, sorry stuff. Each serving consisted of a tin dish containing a lump of gristle and some unidentifiable bones, all of it submerged in rancid grease, and seasoned with the hottest spices I have ever tasted; a tin plate heaped high with stone-cold boiled rice, to which a gram or so of sand had been cunningly added; and a thin, flat piece of unleavened bread about a foot square, as tough as leather and completely flavorless.

The food had other remarkable properties as well – less than five minutes after we had finished eating, our stomachs went into violent, excruciating convulsions, and we raced for the bog, a tiny cubicle at the rear of the chai-house, and spewed up the entire meal.

The rest of the chai stop we spent sipping milk tea, watching the taxidriver smoke opiated hasheesh in a hubbly-bubbly (not an encouraging sight, with the dodgy mountain roads we were traveling on) and listening to the 'attorney' squeak out a feverish speech on the powers of Islam, the villainy of Indira Gandhi, the fearsomeness of our Pathan traveling companions and his desire to be smuggled into the United States so that he could marry Raquel Welch.

It was past four when the taxi finally pulled out of Landi Kotal. I had long since given up hope of surviving the trip, and my only wish was for a mercifully quick end.

On my one side was the driver, his eyes glazed with opium and cannabinol resins, his mouth open, with Allah-only-knows-what technicolor visions muddling his brain and confounding his senses . . . he drove with one lackadaisical finger hooked round the steering wheel, and he droned a funereal dirge under his breath. On the other side, Peter, fatuously stoned on Mandrax, was slurring out the story of a 'Pommy' (Englishman) who had acted like a 'right cunt' somewhere in Australia, and the terrible, but righteous, fate that had befallen him when he'd crossed some large Aussies. They had 'bashed him up goo'.' Beyond him, Anwer Sayed was immersed in an Urdu-language comic book that featured blazing guns, big-breasted blondes in bathtubs and nightgowns and iron-jawed men – strange reading for an 'important attorney', even in Pakistan, I thought.

Behind me, in the back seat, one of the Pathan ruffians snored loudly, two of the others hee-hawed over some joke, while the fourth kept trying to stroke my neck surreptitiously – whenever I turned around, he jumped back and pretended to be looking out the window.

The sun set spectacularly behind us, a pool of raw reds and dusty purples and crackling yellows over the drab mountains, just as the radiator gave out again, and we pulled off the road in the middle of absolute nowhere . . .

Peter and I were consigning our souls to the Cosmos when, a few moments later, the Afghan mail bus, delayed by two successive flat tires, came roaring into view. We flagged it down, nearly weeping with joy, and flung ourselves and our baggage on board. Even the extortionate fare of twenty rupees for the last few miles into Peshawar did not faze us. We had survived the Khyber – we had made it through.

As we pulled away, the Khyber Taxi was still spouting steam like a dying whale, and the Pathans were looking Mister Sayed over like a bunch of Georgia Teamsters eyeing a lone hippie at the Dixie Pig Drive-In in Waycross . . .

'I wouldn't give a rupee for his chances, mate,' Peter said solemnly.

❀ from *Mountain Gazette* (1976)

Dorothy Pilley | *Mountain Rescue*

There is the remarkable story of the man the search-party could not find. When in despair they went back to Arolla, there he was sitting in the hotel garden. 'Wherever have you been? How did we miss you? Didn't you hear our shouts?' they asked. 'Yes,' replied the benighted one, 'but they sounded so terrible and angry that I hid under a rock until you had gone by!'

✳ from *Climbing Days* (1935)

A Short Walk with Whillans

'Did you spot that great long streak of blood on the road over from Chamonix? Twenty yards long, I'd say.'

The speaker was Don Whillans. We were seated in the little inn at Alpiglen, and Don's aggressive profile was framed against an awe-inspiring backdrop of the Eiger-Nordwand. I reflected that the conversation had become attuned to the environment.

'Probably some unfortunate animal,' I ventured without much conviction.

Whillans' eyes narrowed. 'Human blood,' he said. 'Remember – lass?' (appealing to his wife Audrey). 'I told you to stop the car for a better look. Really turned her stomach, it did. Just when she was getting over the funeral.'

I felt an urge to inquire whose funeral they had attended. There had been several. Every time we went up on the Mont-envers train we passed a corpse going down. I let the question go. It seemed irrelevant, possibly even irreverent.

'Ay, it's a good life,' he mused, 'providing you don't weaken.'

'What happens if you do?'

'They bury you,' he growled, and finished his pint.

Don has that rarest of gifts, the ability to condense a whole paragraph into a single, terse, uncompromising sentence. But there are also occasions when he can become almost lyrical in a macabre sort of way. It depends on the environment.

We occupied a window table in the inn. There were several other tables, and hunched round each of these were groups of shadowy men draped in black cagoules – lean-jawed, grim, uncommunicative characters who spoke in guttural monosyllables and gazed steadfastly towards the window. You only had to glimpse their earnest faces to realize that these men were Eiger Candidates – martyrs for the 'Mordwand'.*

'Look at that big black bastard up there,' Whillans chuckled

* Eiger pseudonym coined by the German press – literally 'Murder Wall'.

dryly, gesturing with his thumb. 'Just waiting to get its claws into you. And think of all the young lads who've sat just where you're sitting now, and come back all tied up in sacks. It makes you think.'

It certainly did. I was beginning to wish I had stayed at Chamonix, funerals or no funerals.

'Take that young blonde over there.' He pointed towards the sturdy Aryan barmaid, who had just replenished his glass. 'I wonder how many dead men she's danced with? All the same,' he concluded after a minute's reflection, 't'wouldn't be a bad way to spend your last night.'

I licked my lips nervously. Don's philosophic discourses are not for the faint-hearted.

One of the Eiger Candidates detached himself from a neighbouring group and approached us with obvious intent. He was red-haired, small and compact, and he looked like a Neanderthal man. This likeness derived from his hunched shoulders, and the way he craned his head forwards like a man who had been struck repeatedly on the crown by a heavy hammer, and through time developed a protective over-growth of skull. His name proved to be Eckhart, and he was a German. Most of them still are.

The odd thing about him was his laugh. It had an uncanny hollow quality. He laughed quite a lot without generating a great deal of warmth, and he wore a twisted grin which seemed to be permanently frozen on to his face. Even Whillans was moved.

'You – going – up?' he inquired.

'Nein,' said Eckhart. 'Nix gutt! . . . You wait here little time, I think . . . Now there is much vatter.' He turned up his coat collar ruefully and laughed. 'Many, many stein fall . . . All day, all night . . . Stein, stein.' He tapped his head significantly and laughed uproariously. 'Two nights we wait at *Tod Bivouac*.' He repeated the name as if relishing its sinister undertones. ('It means Dead Man,' I said to Whillans in a hushed whisper.) 'Always it is nix gutt . . . Vatter, stein . . . Stein, vatter . . . so we go down. It is very funny.'

We nodded sympathetically. It was all a huge joke.

'Our two Kameraden, they go on. They are saying at the

telescopes, one man he has fallen fifty metres. Me? I do not believe this.' (Loud and prolonged laughter from the company.)

'You have looked through the telescope?' I inquired anxiously.

'Nein,' he grinned, 'Not necessary . . . tonight they gain summit . . . tomorrow they descend. And now we will have another beer.'

Eckhart was nineteen. He had already accounted for the North Face of the Matterhorn as a training climb, and he intended to camp at the foot of the Eigerwand until the right conditions prevailed. If necessary, he could wait until October. Like most of his countrymen he was nothing if not thorough, and finding his bivouac-tent did not measure up to his expectations he had hitchhiked all the way back to Munich to secure another one. As a result of this, he had missed the settled spell of weather that had allowed several rivals to complete the route, including the second successful British team, Baillie and Haston, and also the lone Swiss climber, Darbellay, who had thus made the first solo ascent.

'Made of the right stuff, that youngster,' observed Don.

'If you ask me I think he was trying to scare us off,' I suggested. 'Psychological warfare, that's all it is.'

'Wait till we get on the face tomorrow,' said Whillans. 'We'll hear your piece then.'

Shortly after noon the next day we left Audrey behind at Alpiglen, and the two of us set off up the green meadows which girdle the foot of the Eigerwand. Before leaving, Don had disposed of his Last Will and Testament. 'You've got the car-key, lass, and you know where to find the house-key. That's all you need to know. Ta, for now.'

Audrey smiled wanly. She had my profound sympathy.

The heat was oppressive, the atmosphere heavy with menace. How many Munich Bergsteigers had trod this very turf on their upward path never to return to their native Klettergarten? I was humming Wagner's *Valkyrie* theme music as we reached the lowest rocks of the Face.

Then a most unexpected thing happened. From an alcove in the wall emerged a very ordinary Swiss tourist, followed by his very ordinary wife, five small children and a poodle dog. I stopped humming immediately. I had read of tearful farewells with wives and sweethearts calling plaintively, but this was ridiculous. What an undignified send-off! The five children accompanied us up the first snow slope scrambling happily in our wake, and prodding our rucksacks with inquisitive fingers. 'Go away,' said Whillans irritably, but ineffectively. We were quite relieved when, ultimately, they were recalled to base and we stopped playing Pied Pipers. The dog held on a bit longer, until some well-directed stones sent it on its way. 'Charming, I must say,' remarked Don. I wondered whether Hermann Buhl would have given up on the spot – a most irregular start to an Eiger Epic and probably a bad omen.

We started climbing up the left side of the shattered pillar, a variant of the normal route which had been perfected by Don in the course of several earlier attempts. He was well on his way to becoming the Grand Old Man of Grindelwald, though not through any fault of his own. This was his fourth attempt at the climb and on every previous occasion he had been turned back by bad weather or by having to rescue his rivals. As a result of this he must have spent more hours on the Face than any other British climber.

Don's preparations for the Eiger – meticulous in every other respect – had not included unnecessary physical exertion. While I dragged my weary muscles from Breuil to Zermatt via the Matterhorn he whiled away the days at Chamonix sunbathing at the Plage until opening time. At the Bar Nationale he nightly sank five or six pints of 'heavy', smoked forty cigarettes, persuaded other layabouts to feed the juke box with their last few francs, and amassed a considerable reputation as an exponent of 'Baby Foot', the table football game which is the national sport of France. One day the heat had been sufficiently intense to cause a rush of blood to the head, because he had walked four miles up to the Montenvers following the railway track, and had acquired such enormous blisters that he had to make the return journey by train. He was nevertheless just as fit as he wanted to be, or indeed needed to be.

First impressions of the Eigerwand belied its evil reputation. This was good climbing rock with excellent friction and lots of small incuts. We climbed unroped, making height rapidly.

In fact I was just starting to enjoy myself, when I found the boot . . .

'Somebody's left a boot here,' I shouted to Don.

He pricked up his ears. 'Look and see if there's a foot in it,' he said.

I had picked it up: I put it down again hurriedly.

'Ha! Here's something else – a torn rucksack,' he hissed. 'And here's his waterbottle – squashed flat.'

I had lost my new-found enthusiasm and decided to ignore future foreign bodies. (I even ignored the pun.)

'You might as well start getting used to them now,' advised Whillans. 'This is where they usually glance off, before they hit the bottom.'

He's a cheery character, I thought to myself. To Don, a spade is just a spade – a simple trenching tool used by gravediggers.

At the top of the Pillar we donned our safety helmets. 'One thing to remember on the Eiger,' said Don, 'never look up, or you may need a plastic surgeon.'

His advice seemed superfluous that evening, as we did not hear a single ricochet. We climbed on up, past the Second Pillar and roped up for the traverse across to the Difficult Crack. At this late hour the Crack was streaming with water, so we decided to bivouac while we were still dry. There was an excellent bivouac cave near the foot of the crack.

'I'll have one of your cigarettes,' said Don. 'I've only brought Gauloises.' This was a statement of fact, not a question. There is something about Don's proverbial bluntness that arouses one's admiration. Of such stuff are generals made. We had a short discussion about bivouacking, but eventually I had to agree with his arguments and occupy the outer berth. It would be less likely to induce claustrophobia, or so I gathered.

I was even more aware of the sudden fall in temperature. My ultra-warm Terray *duvet* failed by a single critical inch to meet the convertible bivvy-rucksack which I had borrowed from Joe Brown. It had been designed, so the manufacturers announced, to Joe's personal specifications, and as far as I could judge, to his personal dimensions as well.

Insidiously and from nowhere, it seemed, a mighty thunderstorm built up in the valley less than a mile away. Flashes of lightning lit up the whole Face and grey tentacles of mist crept out of the dusk threatening to envelop our lofty eyrie.

'The girl in the Tourist Office said that a ridge of high pressure occupying the whole of central Europe would last for at least another three days.'

'Charming,' growled Whillans. 'I could give you a better forecast without raising my head.'

'We should be singing Bavarian drinking songs to keep our spirits up,' I suggested. 'How about some Austrian yodelling?'

'They're too fond of dipping in glacier streams . . . that's what does it,' he muttered sleepily.

'Does what?'

'Makes them yodel. All the same, these bloody Austrians.'

The day dawned clear. For once it seemed that a miracle had happened and a major thunderstorm had cleared the Eiger without lodging on the Face. Don remained inscrutable and cautious as ever. Although we were sheltered from any prevailing wind we would have no advance warning of the weather, as our horizons were limited by the Face itself.

There was still a trickle of water coming down the Difficult Crack as Don launched himself stiffly at the first obstacle. Because of our uncertainty about the weather and an argument about who should make breakfast, we had started late. It was 6.30 a.m. and we would have to hurry. He made a bad start by clipping both strands of the double rope to each of the three pitons he found in position. The rope jammed continuously and this was even more disconcerting for me, when I followed carrying both rucksacks. Hanging down the middle of the pitch was an old frayed rope, said to have been abandoned by Mlle Loulou Boulaz, and this kept getting entangled with the ice-axes. By the time I had joined Don at this stance I was breathing heavily and more than usually irritated. We used the excuse to unrope and get back into normal rhythm before tackling the Hinterstoisser. It was easy to find the route hereabouts: you merely followed the pitons. They were planted everywhere with rotting rope loops (apparently used for abseils) attached to most of them. It is a significant insight into human psychology that nobody ever stops to remove superfluous pegs on the Eiger. If nothing else they help to alleviate the sense of utter isolation that fills this vast Face, but they also act as constant reminders of man's ultimate destiny and the pageant of history written into the rock. Other reminders were there in plenty – gloves, socks, ropes, crampons and boots. None of them appeared to have been abandoned with the owners' consent.

The Hinterstoisser Traverse, despite the illustrations of pre-war heroes traversing 'à la Dulfer', is nothing to get excited about. With two fixed ropes of unknown vintage as an emergency handrail, you can walk across it in three minutes. Stripped of scaffolding, it would probably qualify as Severe by contemporary British standards. The fixed ropes continued without a break as far as the Swallow's Nest – another bivouac site hallowed by tradition. Thus far I could well have been climbing the Italian Ridge of the Matterhorn.

We skirted the first icefield on the right, scrambling up easy rubble where we had expected to find black ice. It was certainly abnormally warm, but if the weather held we had definite grounds for assuming that we could complete the climb in one day – our original intention. The Ice Hose which breaches the rocky barrier between the First and Second Icefields no longer merited the name, because the ice had all gone. It seemed to offer an easy alley but Don preferred to stick to known alternatives and advanced upon an improbable-looking wall some distance across to the left. By the time I had confirmed our position on Hiebeler's route description, he had completed the pitch and was shouting for me to come on. He was well into his stride, but still did not seem to share my optimism.

His doubts were well founded. Ten minutes later, we were crossing the waterworn slabs leading on to the Second Icefield when we saw the first falling stones. To be exact we did not see the stones, but merely the puff of smoke each one left behind at the point of impact. They did not come bouncing down the cliff with a noisy clatter as stones usually do. In fact they were only audible after they had gone past – WROUFF! – a nasty sort of sound half-way between a suck and a blow.

'It's the small ones that make that sort of noise,' explained Whillans. 'Wait till you hear the really big ones!'

The blueprint for a successful Eiger ascent seems to involve being at the right place at the right time. According to our calculations the Face should have been immune to stonefall at this hour of the morning.

Unfortunately the Eiger makes its own rules. An enormous black cloud had taken shape out of what ought to have been a clear blue sky, and had come to rest on the summit icefield. It reminded me of a gigantic black vulture spreading its wings before dropping like lightning on unsuspecting prey.

Down there at the foot of the Second Icefield, it was suddenly very cold and lonely. Away across to the left was the Ramp; a possible hideaway to sit out the storm. It seemed little more than a stone's throw, but I knew as well as Don did that we had almost 1,500 feet of steep snow-ice to cross before we could get any sort of shelter from stones.

There was no question of finding adequate cover in the immediate vicinity. On either side of us steep ice slopes, peppered with fallen debris, dropped away into the void. Simultaneously with Whillans' arrival at the stance the first flash of lightning struck the White Spider.

'That settles it,' said he, clipping the spare rope through my belay karabiner.

'What's going on?' I demanded, finding it hard to credit that such a crucial decision could be reached on the spur of the moment.

'I'm going down,' he said. 'That's what's going on.'

'Wait a minute! Let's discuss the whole situation calmly.' I stretched out one hand to flick the ash off my cigarette. Then a most unusual thing happened. There was a higher-pitched 'wrouff' than usual and the end of my cigarette disappeared! It was the sort of subtle touch that Hollywood film directors dream about.

'I see what you mean,' I said. 'I'm going down too.'

I cannot recall coming off a climb so quickly. As a result of a long acquaintance Don knew the location of every abseil point, and this enabled us to bypass the complete section of the climb which includes the Hinterstoisser Traverse and the Chimney leading up to the Swallow's Nest. To do this, you merely rappel directly downwards from the last abseil point above the

Swallow's Nest and so reach a key piton at the top of the wall overlooking the start of the Hinterstoisser Traverse. From here a straightforward rappel of 140 feet goes vertically down the wall to the large ledge at the start of the Traverse. If Hinterstoisser had realized that he would probably not now have a Traverse named after him, and the Eigerwand would not enjoy one half its present notoriety. The idea of 'a Point of No Return' always captures the imagination, and until very recent times it was still the fashion to abandon a fixed rope at the Hinterstoisser in order to safeguard a possible retreat.

The unrelenting bombardment, which had kept us hopping from one abseil to the next like demented fleas, began to slacken off as we came into the lee of the 'Rote Fluh'. The weather had obviously broken down completely and it was raining heavily. We followed separate ways down the easy lower section of the Face, sending down volleys of loose scree in front of us. Every now and again we heard strange noises, like a series of muffled yelps, but since we appeared to have the mountain to ourselves, this did not provoke comment. Whillans had just disappeared round a nearby corner when I heard a loud ejaculation.

'God Almighty,' he said (or words to that effect). 'Japs! Come and see for yourself!'

Sure enough, there they were. Two identical little men in identical climbing uniforms, sitting side by side underneath an overhang. They had been crouching there for an hour, waiting for the bombardment to slacken. I estimated that we must have scored several near misses.

'You – Japs?' grunted Don. It seemed an unnecessary question.

'Yes, yes,' they grinned happily, displaying a full set of teeth. 'We are Japanese.'

'Going – up?' queried Whillans. He pointed meaningfully at the grey holocaust sweeping down from the White Spider.

'Yes, yes,' they chorused in unison. 'Up. Always upwards. First Japanese Ascent.'

'You-may-be-going-up-Mate,' said Whillans, giving every syllable unnecessary emphasis, 'but-a-lot-'igher-than-you-think!'

They did not know what to make of this, so they wrung his hand several times, and thanked him profusely for the advice.

' 'Appy little pair!' said Don. 'I don't imagine we'll ever see them again.'

He was mistaken. They came back seven days later after several feet of new snow had fallen. They had survived a full-scale Eiger blizzard and had reached our highest point on the Second Icefield. If they did not receive a medal for valour they had certainly earned one. They were the forerunners of the climbing élite of Japan, whose members now climb Mount Everest for the purpose of ski-ing back down again.

We got back to the Alpiglen in time for late lunch. The telescope stood forlorn and deserted in the rain. The Eiger had retired into its misty oblivion, as Don Whillans retired to his favourite corner seat by the window.

✻ from *One Man's Mountains* (1971)

G. D. Abraham | *Strong Chap,*
| *Jones*

In climbing steep couloirs, zigzags enable the rock-walls to be used now and again as anchorage – a point specially to be noted amongst the Chamonix aiguilles, where a sudden slip may occur. Owen Glynne Jones once saved a whole party of well-known experts on such an occasion. In descending a steep icy gully on the Aiguille du Plan one of the party of four slipped; an avalanche started and all were dragged off with terrific suddenness. Luckily Jones, who was last man down, with instant presence of mind, was able to jam his ice-axe lengthwise across a narrow rock rift, and with the rope over this he was able to hold grimly on and stem the mad rush to destruction. Nothing much was said at the time; later on one of the experts was heard to remark: 'Strong chap, that fellow Jones!' That was all.

※ from *Modern Mountaineering* (1933)

William Howarth | *Wildmen*

Like a reflection coalesces when roiled water stills, the Bear's sweaty face emerges out of the tapestry of green, cheek striped with blood, shirt ripped, one leg of his Levis torn. I'm in about the same shape. My shirt is in strips and there are deep scratches on my hands and arms. Mopping his face with his bandana, the Bear says 'We're off the route, Ivan.'

'What route? Hell with this, Bear. Let's go back.'

Watery blue eyes reflecting the green, he grins, says 'It's gonna thin out', and I know, typical of the Bear, that this adversity has fuelled his enthusiasm.

We hadn't at the start had much. We'd dawdled over breakfast, listened to the weather report – continued hot – and to an account of how tourists picnicking on the Hamma Hamma, the next major drainage north from where we are right now, had encountered, they said, the ape-like, abominable snowman of North America, the notorious Sasquatch or Bigfoot. All that summer people up and down the coast had been seeing him, but this was the first sighting in the Eastern Olympics of Washington State.

We hadn't left my house in Olympia till after eight, so it was nearly ten when we pulled up on the Jefferson Lake Road about half a mile past the lake and gazed at the mountain, its southern slopes rising to what seemed an easy snowfall on to rock to the summit ridge. 'It's a snap,' the Bear had said. 'Let's go home and say we done it.'

Over the years we had climbed all the biggies that front on the Hood Canal of Puget Sound – Ellinor, Washington, Cruiser, Stone, The Brothers, Constance and so on. Even Baldy and Bretherton. The only peak remaining of any consequence was this one, Pershing (6,154), which lies just due north of Mt Washington. A push-over, we figured. A chore. We didn't even bother to consult the *Climber's Guide to the Olympic Range*. So when the Bear had called me at work on Thursday during early July and proposed it for that Saturday I had agreed more out of an obligation to complete our record than anything else.

This particular Bear, Donald G. Thomas of Tumwater, is stark evidence for reincarnation – his regeneration from Bear to man having been only partially completed. He looks and acts like a Bear.

From the roadhead we'd travelled easily up Jefferson Creek for a mile or so to a tiny lake, then, forced by steep rock laced with waterfalls, we cut due west, heading for an inviting open strip of green higher up. Easy at first it was, but now for more than two hours we've been literally climbing over and around house-sized boulders through old growth willow and vine maple intermixed with stumps and parts of trees avalanched off higher ground. It's like being where God threw all the leftover stuff after making the mountains, although I wouldn't want to blame it on Him. Half the time, we've been off the ground.

'You think we'll hit the open pretty soon, uh?' I say, still feeling no enthusiasm as we stand on what I think is the ground, a wall surrounding us of salal, vine maple, blackberry, huckle-berry, salmonberry, Devil's club, alder, bracken, poison oak, nettles, saplings, blowdowns.

'It can't go on for ever,' the Bear says.

'I'm not so sure.' I've been feeling it was for ever. You've heard of mile-a-day country. Well, this is half-a-mile-a-day, if that. 'Think we've made any progress?' I say, turning to the Bear, but the Bear is gone, dissolved again into the green wall. For a moment I'm confused about which way, till I hear him cursing and thrashing and I follow, using my body like a battering ram, pushing a cord of vine maple out of my way. 'Thwack,' it whips back and slices my cheek.

At one point we hit an alder thicket where the saplings grow like fence rails. Mosquitoes eat us. Fifteen on your face, sweat in your eyes, a branch poking your kidney, nettles stinging, dust gritty between your teeth, your foot twisted and you can't move because your rucksack is hung up on something, your right hand has to keep a branch from springing back in your face and your other hand must thread your ice-axe through the maze. It takes ten minutes to extricate yourself. No torture of the

Inquisition could be more fiendish. One time, caught together in one of these – we call them 'jackpots' – the Bear, with sweat-grinning face, says 'Ivan, explain why we're here?' He's right. We could be watching the ball game and drinking beer. I swear I would've given anything for a beer, especially when, famished from putting out so much energy, we tore into the lunch we'd brought in the one rucksack we traded off carrying.

Shortly after lunch the Bear bumbles into a patch of Devil's club and gets a hand so full of thorns it takes fifteen minutes to pick them out.

It is after two when, cut, bruised and practically shorn of shirts, we emerge on to the rock. It's no picnic, either. Low down is scree of the you-know, one-step-forward-for-every-two-back variety. Like Sisyphus in Hades condemned eternally to roll a stone uphill only to have it roll down, we get nowhere. To add to our frustration, from fairly high up we determine there is no way back that avoids the brush.

Higher, up in the cirque on Pershing's south side, we get into steep snow – a relief after the brush – and then, when we thought we had it made – into pillow lava that comes out in handfuls and breaks off underfoot in chunks. We stick together, the mountain smoking with dust behind us and roaring with avalanches we couldn't help starting.

At one point the Bear gets ahead of me and I hear him yell 'Sonofabitch . . .' followed by what sounds like a rockfall. Dust rises against the sun. I haul myself over the rockpile that blocks my view to see tumbling head over heels and coming to rest like a discarded doll, arms and legs outstretched, face to the ground, the Bear. 'Oh, Gawd, he's done,' I think, hollering, 'Y' all right, Bear?'

No answer. Lifeless form below. If he's alive, I figure, starting down, he's in shock. Gotta keep him warm. Go down to the Guard Station. Get a helicopter. Be morning before they can get in here. Jeezus, can't be too cold tonight with this hot weather.

'Don. Y' all right?'

No movement.

My legs are shaking. 'Jeezus. Don?'

'What?'

I almost can't believe it's his voice. 'You hurt, Don?'

He sits bolt upright. 'No, goddammit.'

The chute is like a slide when you were a kid. The Bear had stopped on the run-out, a pile of scree. A white, hairy leg glares at me like the patches of him that show through his shirt. His pant-leg is split from ankle to crotch. Levis, they sure don't make them like they used to, I think. He makes his way up, bare knee flashing in and out of the torn pant-leg, one dusty testicle protruding from the slit. Because of the chafing they give on hot, sweaty climbs, neither of us is graced with the nicety of underpants.

Apart from abrasions, the Bear is not hurt. His blue eyes flash at the summit. 'Sonofabitch. It wants our clothes.'

We negotiate a snow steep that brings us to the ridge crest, where we stand looking downrange. The Hood Canal glitters in the haze. Don's pant-leg flaps in the light breeze and our tattered shirts threaten to blow away. The seat of my pants is out. So is the Bear's. Even his bandana is gone. We are also both nauseous from too much cold water and starting to get leg cramps because of copious sweating. Naturally, for a pushover like Pershing, we didn't bring salt tablets. It's quarter to five.

By the time we reach the summit we are both half naked. Our record is complete. It is nearly 6.30. We might have a chance to get out of the brush before dark. We might.

Down we go, riding the avalanches, peeling off snow steeps, skidding into scree run-outs, shredding our clothes and our skins even more. Already the cirque is in the mountain's deep shadow. What a sight we are – red faces, white bodies. Reaching the maze of green we thrash about. The faster we try to go, the more jackpots we get into. At one point, on a vertical pitch, we lower ourselves in trees from limb to limb over creeks and waterfalls. Fun when you have leg cramps. We can barely see by the time I stop at a seep on more level ground and holler at the Bear. He comes crashing through the salal. 'What?'

I can hardly make out his face. 'Let's bivouac till first light.'

With my pocket knife I cut some of the brush and we lie back under a scatter of stars visible through the canopy of foliage, the silence broken only by our slaps at mosquitoes. I sleep, wake up cold, lean over the moss by the seep and strike a match and check my watch. One twenty. Thank God it's a short night. We talk, occasionally slipping into sleep. Pretty soon we're both shivering. It's 3.30. About the time I can make out the dial on my watch the mosquitoes move in. The Bear does a dance to keep them off and stay warm. I swat endlessly. The outlines of trees appear. Then the green closes in and after a drink from the seep, we move out.

Nothing went right that morning. First off, the Bear's remaining pant-leg strips off when he scales a slick, up-ended log and loses his balance and skids back down it into the dense huckleberry he'd tried to bridge via the log. Second, my cotton pants, a holdover from the navy, don't survive what seems like the millionth berry patch. By this time, of course, our shirts are gone. I use a remnant of mine as a loin cloth. A lot of these shreds of clothing were lost because we didn't miss them until

'. . . then turn and like stricken deer bolt across in front of the car and into the tapestry of green . . .'

we happened to look at ourselves, which we didn't have time to do very often. If you tied a piece to you, as in the case of my loin cloth, it would be ripped off, and no way would you fight the thicket or climb the log again to get it back. When the rucksack with our crampons in it ripped off my back, though, I did go looking for it. Couldn't find it. Thus the green beast mauled us all the way to the road.

I don't say to the truck because we had, of course – Pershing being a snap – no compass (we'd lost our topo), and so got clear off the – what shall I call It? 'Route' seems inappropriate – the straight line. We came to the road a mile or so, we figured, below the truck.

We carry our axes and have our boots on. That's it.

I experience the joy of simply walking unhindered. The Bear grabs my arm. 'Hey, Ivan. What if a car comes?'

He's right. This is civilization. We're naked. 'We'll duck into the brush,' I tell him. 'Nobody uses this road.'

In a jovial mood, we tie vine maple to us and drape leaves and wispy lengths of Spanish moss from what grows out over the road and move fast, padding in thick dust, the beast at bay on either side.

We get to joking – 'the Bear is bare,' and so on – and don't notice as we round a curve that on the side of the road that we're on there's a drop-off. So when a car appears at the curve and is suddenly upon us we do a dance on the edge and then turn and like stricken deer bolt across in front of the car and into the tapestry of green on the other side, giving them, I'm sure, just a glimpse of us. We're getting good at this, I think, crawling behind the Bear, pushing, ploughing, rolling over a log, lying together, panting.

The motor stops. Voices, male and female. We can't hear distinctly because of a nearby creek. People walk in the brush. Then there is quiet. Finally, the car starts. Gears grind. The motor roars.

'They're turning around,' the Bear hisses, bear-like face close to mine.

'Wonder why?'

We found out why when, after getting to the truck without further incident and finding not only trousers but a couple of scroungy shirts, we drive out. At the Hamma Hamma Guard Station are two state patrol cars and a crowd. A forest service guy the Bear knows as Mike spills out a tale that makes us stare at each other in such amazement that, leaning his elbows on the door of the truck, Mike says, 'Don't tell me you guys saw it, too?'

The gist of it is that a family from L A – Mike points them out talking to the patrolmen – has seen, he says, 'not just one, but two hairy, kinda pale-looking wildmen dressed in leaves running across the road up near Jefferson Lake. They was carrying spears.'

In the Olympia paper that Monday there was a spread about it. Being upright citizens and conscientious guys, we decide to tell all and so drove over to the paper after work Tuesday. Paunchy, in short sleeves with necktie knot pulled loose, the reporter's protruding brown eyes roll over us. The story when we tell it sounds crazy.

'How can plants tear your clothes off?'

'Ever been in the brush in the Olympics?' the Bear says.

The man hadn't. Not the outdoorsy type, he tells us, and I realize he really doesn't know what the hell we're talking about. I make the mistake of calling Don 'the Bear'. The guy narrows his eyes. 'Hey,' he says, 'I'd really like to believe you guys, you know, but there've been two similar sightings in the area since Saturday – took the calls myself – one late Sunday, the other just this morning describing creatures dressed in vegetation. I'm working on a front-page story right now' – he seems anxious, I think, to get back to this. 'Wildmen,' he says, eyes sticking out. 'Wildmen – or mebbee some Bigfoot albinos.'

'Bushwhacked,' the Bear mumbles.

That September there were several more wildmen spotted in separate parts of Western Washington. The feature magazine of the Seattle paper ran an article on the sightings (wildmen and Sasquatch) and, still trying to set this record straight too, we wrote a letter to the editor. Even written, our story sounded crazy. The letter was never printed.

Then, in late fall, the familiar, hairy old Sasquatch himself starts appearing again and making the papers. Everybody forgets about wildmen.

The Bear, however, determined to make something out of the whole episode, is claiming the first nude ascent of Pershing.
I suspect it's not the first.

✻ from *Climber and Rambler* (1975)

S. Russell Jones | *In Nepal*

'The Package Deal to Everest's Summit is not far off . . .
The Nepalese, only their culture and ecology suffer.'
Peter Boardman (*Mountain*, December 1980)

Are the Travel Agents checking
                In Nepal
On the hordes of tourists trekking
                In Nepal?
Does the traffic cause congestion
On the way up from Darjeeling?
Will some Walker ask the question
'Do you ever get the feeling
Solitude has lost its meaning?'
Leader, read the Writing on the Wall!
Chomolungma must be keening
                In Nepal.

Himalayan altars cluster
                In Nepal
Where the flocks of trippers muster
                In Nepal.
Will they witness Crowd Euphoria
When, to cater for the masses,
Woolworth opens chain emporia –
Cook's Tours cope with Kukri Classes?
Beauty Queen, Miss Nanda Devi
Yet may call with Stuart Hall.
(Bumbust bombast laid on heavy)
                In Nepal.

Will the Cubs and Brownies rally
                In Nepal?
Will they squeak 'Ayo Gurkhali'
                In Nepal?
Will some Rhondda Valley boyo

Take on tour a Welsh Fifteen –
Build a Grandstand on Cho Oyo
Just to dominate the scene?
Will some millionaire like Getty
Bid for Lhotse's silver shawl?
– Butlin rent a Redcoat Yeti

                              In Nepal?

Will the Disco Dhaulagiri

                              In Nepal

Keep the Happy Campers cheery

                              In Nepal?

Cable cars on Kangchenjunga . . .
Charter Flights round Makalu . . .
Gunga Dins with Gin or Younger
Served in Bars on Manaslu . . .

          Pioneers of High Safari
Will they sigh 'God save us all',
Pipe an eye and cry 'Peccavi'

                              In Nepal?

❀ from *Climber and Rambler* (1982)

Mark Twain | An Ascent of the Riffelberg

As usual at Zermatt when a great ascent is about to be undertaken, everybody, native and foreign, laid aside his own projects and took up a good position to observe the start. The expedition consisted of 198 persons, including the mules, or 205, including the cows. As follows:

Chiefs of Service	*Subordinates*
Myself	1 Veterinary Surgeon
Mr Harris	1 Butler
17 Guides	12 Waiters
4 Surgeons	1 Footman
1 Geologist	1 Barber
1 Botanist	1 Head Cook
3 Chaplains	9 Assistants
2 Draftsmen	4 Pastry Cooks
15 Barkeepers	1 Confectionary Artist
1 Latinist	

Transportation, etc.

27 Porters	3 Coarse Washers and Ironers
44 Mules	1 Fine ditto.
44 Muleteers	7 Cows
	2 Milkers

Total, 154 men, 51 animals. Grand Total, 205

It was full four o'clock in the afternoon before my cavalcade was entirely ready. At that hour it began to move. In point of numbers and spectacular effect it was the most imposing expedition that had ever marched from Zermatt.

I commanded the chief guide to arrange the men and animals in single file, twelve feet apart, and lash them all together on a strong rope. He objected that the first two miles was a dead level, with plenty of room, and that the rope was never used except in very dangerous places. But I would not listen to that.

My reading had taught me that many serious accidents had happened in the Alps simply from not having the people tied up soon enough; I was not going to add one to the list. The guide then obeyed my order.

When the procession stood at ease, roped together and ready to move, I never saw a finer sight. It was 3,122 feet long – over half a mile; every man but Harris and me was on foot, and had on his green veil and his blue goggles, and his white rag round his hat, and his coil of rope over one shoulder and under the other, and his ice-axe in his belt, and carried his alpenstock in his left hand, his umbrella (closed) in his right, and his crutches slung at his back. The burdens of the pack mules and the horns of the cows were decked with the Edelweiss and the Alpine rose.

I and my agent were the only persons mounted. We were in the post of danger in the extreme rear, and tied securely to five guides apiece. Our armour-bearers carried our ice-axes, alpenstocks and other implements for us. We were mounted upon very small donkeys, as a measure of safety; in time of peril we could straighten our legs and stand up, and let the donkey walk from under. Still, I cannot recommend this sort of animal – at least for excursions of mere pleasure – because his ears interrupt the view. I and my agent possessed the regulation mountaineering costumes, but concluded to leave them behind. Out of respect for the great numbers of tourists of both sexes who would be assembled in front of the hotels to see us pass, and also out of respect for the many tourists whom we expected to encounter on our expedition, we decided to make the ascent in evening dress.

At fifteen minutes past four I gave the command to move, and my subordinates passed it along the line. The great crowd in front of the Monte Rosa Hotel parted in twain, with a cheer, as the procession approached, and as the head of it was filing by I gave the order 'Unlimber – make ready – HOIST!' and with one impulse up went my half-mile of umbrellas. It was a beautiful sight, and a total surprise to the spectators. Nothing like that had ever been seen in the Alps before. The applause it brought forth was deeply gratifying to me, and I rode by with my plug hat in my hand to testify my appreciation of it.

It was the only testimony I could offer, for I was too full to speak . . .

Toward nightfall, when we were about tired out, we came up against a rock as big as a cottage. This barrier took all the remaining spirit out of the men, and a panic of fear and despair ensued. They moaned and wept, and said they should never see their homes and their dear ones again. Then they began to upbraid me for bringing them upon this fatal expedition. Some even muttered threats against me.

But when the danger was most imminent, we were saved in a mysterious way. A mule, which had attracted attention from the beginning by its disposition to experiment, tried to eat a five-pound can of nitro-glycerine. This happened right alongside the rock. The explosion threw us all to the ground, and covered us with dirt and debris; it frightened us extremely, too, for the crash it made was deafening, and the violence of the shock made the ground tremble. However, we were grateful, for the rock was gone. Its place was occupied by a new cellar, about thirty feet across by fifteen feet deep. The explosion was heard as far as Zermatt; and an hour and a half afterwards many citizens of that town were knocked down and quite seriously injured by descending portions of mule meat, frozen solid. This shows, better than any estimate in figures, how high the experimenter went . . .

We followed the mule road, a zigzag course, now to the right, now to the left, but always up, and always crowded and incommoded by going and coming files of reckless tourists who were never, in a single instance, tied together. I was obliged to exert the utmost care and caution, for in many places the road was not two yards wide, and often the lower side of it sloped away in slanting precipices eight and even nine feet deep. I had to encourage the men constantly, to keep them from giving way to their unmanly fears.

We might have made the summit before night but for a delay caused by the loss of an umbrella. I was for allowing the umbrella to remain lost, but the men murmured, and with reason, for in this exposed region we stood in peculiar need of protection against avalanches; so I went into camp and detached a strong party to go after the missing article.

The difficulties of next morning were severe, but our courage was high, for our goal was near. At noon we conquered the last impediment – we stood at last upon the summit – and without the loss of a single man, except the mule that ate the nitro-glycerine. Our great achievement was achieved – the possibility of the impossible was demonstrated, and Harris and I walked proudly into the great dining-room of the Riffelberg Hotel and stood our alpenstocks up in a corner.

❋ from *A Tramp Abroad* (1880)

Frederick Burlingham | *True Grit*

A little to the left was the theatre of another tragic accident which caused the death of three Englishmen and a Chamonix guide. There were six in the party, and having arrived at the col, were descending a snow slope on the Italian side by the side of the rocks which are usually followed. All that is known to the public is that the two men who led and followed the party let go the rope and escaped, while the three Englishmen and Tairraz went to destruction. Tairraz screamed, but, like Englishmen, the others met their doom without a word of exclamation.

from *How To Become An Alpinist* (1914)

Mike Thompson | *Out with the Boys Again*

Our leader had decreed that, in order not to place an intolerable burden upon the Nepalese countryside, we should walk to Base Camp in two parties, one travelling a day behind the other. Perhaps unwisely, he labelled these the 'A team' and the 'B team', and immediately there was much speculation as to the underlying basis for his selection. At first there were fears among the B team that the choice of summiters had already taken place and that they were travelling with the leader in order that they could plot the fine details of the assault in secrecy. But even the most paranoid could not sustain this belief for long, and a more popular theory was that the 'chaps' were in the A team and the 'lads' in the B team. This perhaps was nearer the truth since what had happened was that Chris had, quite understandably, taken with him all the executives: Sirdar Pertemba, Base Camp Manager Mike Cheney, Equipment Officer Dave Clarke, Senior Doctor Charles Clarke, and of course the media in the shape of the *Sunday Times* reporter and the television team. These middle managers were, during their fortnight's walk, to have the interesting experience of, in the words of Our Leader, 'being let in on his thinking'. The B team, gloriously free of logistics, planning, scenarios, computer print-outs, communication set-ups and the like, immediately sank into that form of communal warmth generated by squaddies in a barrack room, that impenetrable bloody-mindedness born of the I-only-work-here mentality of the shop-floor. A series of perfectly sensible decisions led to the emphasis of a division that is always incipiently present in any large expedition. The A team represented the Overground Leadership, the B team the Underground Leadership.

In theory, we, the B team members, were in the tender care of the Deputy Dawg, Hamish MacInnes, but Hamish is never one to assert his authority unduly and even if he had tried to he

would have had to cope with that powerfully built and passionate anarchist, Doug Scott. One of the disadvantages of anarchy
concerns decision-making. For myself, I always feel that too
much fuss is made about decisions on expeditions. There seems
to me to be only one real decision, which is when that letter in
unmistakable scrawl arrives, saying: 'How about coming on the
coldest holiday of your life. PS Will you do the food?', and like
a fool you write back and say 'Yes'. But on the day the A team
left Kathmandu, Deputy Dawg fell ill. Should we set off the next
day as planned, leaving Hamish behind, or should we wait a
few days to see if he recovered – a course of action (or, rather,
inaction) that might also allow Martin Boysen, who had got his
leg stuck in the Trango Tower, to catch up with us? Of course,
Hamish himself should have taken the decision, but he, though
unable to walk, refused to admit that he was ill. His Scottish
stubbornness is so highly developed that even if he had a leg
amputated he would insist that it was just a slight limp. Not one
of us was prepared to take that enormous step from private
soldier to lance corporal, and make a decision, so several
delightful days were passed in the fleshpots of Kathmandu until
very early one morning some Land Rovers arrived at the hotel.
They seemed to be for us, so we set off.

I suppose that during the approach we should have been
organized by the second Sirdar, Ang Phu, but he had been
having severe marital problems and was hitting the chang pretty
hard, so we just wandered along, stopping where the Sherpas
usually stopped, eating what Kancha the cook gave us to eat
and generally building up a casual yet strong rapport with the
Sherpas, by approving of their choice of camp-sites and menus,
and by luring one another into wayside chang-houses.

The members of the A team had adopted the puritanical
regime of getting up in the morning, eating breakfast, and then
walking until they got to the next camp-site in the afternoon.
We followed the more traditional pattern of just tea and biscuits
in bed, followed by two or three hours' walk during the cool of
early morning, until, rounding a corner, one came across the
kitchen with its alfresco breakfast of pancakes, eggs, chips,
cheese, tuna fish, tea and chocolate biscuits, almost ready to
serve. After this a little sleep and a gentle run-in through a few

chang-houses would bring us to the next camp-site in the early afternoon. Of course there were occasional interruptions to the idyllic progress of this mobile, intensive-care geriatric unit, such as when Doug Scott was waylaid at a chang-house by Ang Phu before the sun had even risen and never even reached the breakfast place, or when I foolishly followed Ned Kelly (who had been there before) and ended up in a trackless jungle and on the wrong side of a monsoon-swollen torrent.

The level of conversation was exceptionally high, by which I mean that we gave full rein to a very childish brand of humour, often in questionable taste. The greatest favourites were Whillans Jokes. One could always tell when one of these was coming as the teller would suddenly screw up his face, narrow his eyes to slits and begin to emit a high-pitched whine. Useful on many occasions, to justify the imbalance between a porter carrying about 70 lb. and a sahib carrying his Olympus OM 1, was: 'No! No! These fellows are used to it – they've done it all their lives.' Happy hours were passed recounting those epics in which Whillans would gradually unfold an account of his rectitude and forbearance in the face of seemingly intolerable chicanery and provocation. Like some Greek tragedy the sequence of events would move inexorably to the inevitable, fateful conclusion. All such tales led to the same final and literal punch-line: 'So I 'it 'im.'

Hamish MacInnes recounted how, during Dr Herrligkoffer's European Expedition to the South-West Face of Everest, Don, apart from nicknaming his leader 'Sterlingscoffer', did in fact behave with astonishing forbearance in the face of almost unendurable provocation and never once stepped out of line – *until the expedition was over.*

Apparently, during the earliest stages of the expedition, when the members were just getting to know one another, they heard on the Base Camp radio that Germany had just beaten England in the World Cup. 'Aha!' cried the dour Felix Kuen (the climbing leader) to Don, 'we have beaten you at your national game!' Don paused, looked around, narrowed his eyes to the merest slits, leant forward, paused again and said in a harsh whisper: 'Aye, but we've beaten you at your national game twice now.' No wonder the individualistic, subversive Whillans became the cult hero of the B team. Never was anyone more present by his absence.

The other great approach-march sport, I'm ashamed to say, was 'Boardman-baiting'. Poor Peter had recently been appointed to the post of Permanent Under-Secretary to the President of the National Amalgamated Union of Mountaineers of Great Britain and Bradford. What is more, he alone amongst us was being paid while on the expedition: somewhere, we believed, in the region of £30,000 per year, of our, the taxpayers' money. The reality was barely less infuriating: he was the National Officer of the British Mountaineering Council (the BMC), which as you will all know is run by Dennis Gray, who, on several occasions (on the basis of his experience on some very large expeditions to quite small mountains), has attacked modest expeditions (including ours) to very large mountains as being counter to the proletarian ideology of the true heartland and fountain-head of British Mountaineering – Yorkshire.

But perhaps, while on the subject of Yorkshire, I can digress for a moment, for we did have with us one Yorkshireman, Mike Rhodes (from Bradford, to boot). Mike had not, until Everest came along, travelled outside Yorkshire. After all, what is there outside Yorkshire worth travelling for? Whenever anything un-Yorkshire-like happened to him, such as being bitten by a leech, being offered curry and rice, spaghetti and Parmesan cheese or chang, or falling through a crevasse in the ice-fall, he would remark in a surprised and slightly pained voice: 'Nothing like this in Bradford' (pronounced 'Bratfud'). As Martin Boysen remarked, when he finally caught us up: 'People are always going on about the dangers of professional mountaineers, but what about professional Yorkshiremen?'

But to return to Boardman-baiting: this would usually be initiated by some seemingly innocent inquiry such as 'What do you do all day in your office on the fiftieth floor of Dennis Gray Tower?' And then we would hear about all sorts of official bodies, such as the UIAA and the MLC Board, about negotiations for access, about grant supports for students writing PhDs on climbing harnesses or crash-hats and reading papers on specialized aspects of their research at international seminars in the Caucasus. All this was a revelation to me: I had been climbing all these years unaware of the existence of this bureaucracy, and it was all I could do to keep up with the initials and the jargon. Crags, I discovered, were 'recreational facilities' and the BMC was empowered, if need be, to acquire these recreational facilities by compulsory purchase (CPO, you know). And all this time I'd thought they were crags!

> Recreational Facility of Ages, cleft for me,
> Let me hide myself in Thee.

Usually, by this time, Tut would be writhing on the ground in paroxysms of laughter, gasping: 'PhDs on harness, BSI kite-marked nuts'; and Doug, fists clenched and beads of sweat standing out on his furrowed brow, would be dreaming of the not-too-far-off day when he would lead his first guerrilla raid to blow up a National Park Information Centre; or the glorious morning when the newspaper headlines would shriek: 'Stanage Warden Murdered By Inadequately Clad Climber.'

If the baiting was taking place in a chang-house, the chances were that it would really take off at this point, the British Mountaineering Council becoming one with the British Motor Corporation and Dennis Gray merging with Lord Stokes and being blamed for the state of the economy and for mini-vans breaking down on the M1. And then, in a desperate conciliatory gesture Peter would deliver the final stunning blow: 'But we're doing all this *on your behalf.*'

At Kunde, we momentarily met up with the A team. Though we were forced to attend an expedition meeting ('Welcome aboard,' said Our Leader, adopting the terminology of the only one of the armed services of which he has not been a member) and to perform the more menial tasks of equipment-issue and crampon-adjustment, we did have the rare pleasure of watching Dave Clarke as he presided over the most depressing thing that can happen to any shopkeeper – the distribution of his entire stock without receiving a penny in exchange. There was a brief respite when we split again into A and B teams for the walk to Base Camp, but once there the Underground Leadership was totally submerged as The Logistic Machine swung into action – and very impressive action it was too! We got our kicks in the Ice-fall – up at two in the morning and glissade down in time

for breakfast – and did penance trying to break down the MacInnes boxes into 30 lb. loads: all the sections of the incredibly complicated aluminium frames were threaded together with elastic string and, just as one coaxed the last bit into a large cardboard box, another bit would escape and the whole frame would re-erect itself like a monstrous Jack-in-the-box. It was more than even Boysen's legendary patience could stand and the Old Fox of Glencoe's ears must have been burning as, far above us in the Western Cwm, he indulged himself constructing the highest truss-girder bridge in the world.

The Sherpas built a shrine to placate whatever it was that lived in the Ice-fall and consecrated it with McVitie's chocolate wholemeal biscuits and John Haig Whisky; and Mr and Mrs Boardman (Dim Juff, the Duff Doctor) excavated outside their tent a patio-cum-sun-terrace which, with its genteel folding chairs and sun-shaded table, might have passed unremarked on the Algarve, but had a certain incongruity at eighteen-and-a-half thousand feet on the Khumbu Glacier.

At this early stage of the climb there were far too many Chiefs and far too many Indians, and this, coupled with the fact that there was only one camp and that all the action took place within full view of it, meant that the traditional avenues whereby the Underground Leadership could assert its devious influence were firmly closed. Usually, on such expeditions, the Overground Leadership can be contained by witchcraft accusations, of which the most feared (and therefore most effective) are 'secret-eating' and 'equipment-hoarding'. 'Unnatural sexual practices' is, by comparison, surprisingly ineffective. On the positive side, the Underground can, once the expedition is strung out over a number of camps and communications are strained, influence the course of events by withholding information. In this way the Overground still makes all the decisions, but on the basis of grossly inadequate information, and this means that, skilfully handled, the Overground without realizing it simply okays the wishes of the Underground. When communications are really stretched it may be possible to ignore the Overground completely and present them with, in Mick Burke's phrase, 'a *fait accompli*, as they say in Spain'. For this kind of action to be constructive in the long run, one needs a leader who changes his mind a lot and has difficulty in remembering from one day to the next what he has decided. We were fortunate in having such a leader.

Once on the face itself, the situation suddenly changed. It was like Annapurna again: all at once the expedition was quite small; there weren't enough people to do everything that had to be done and one's own contributions and omissions were immediately evident to one's fellows. At last, this was what we had come for!

The fulfilment of long-cherished desires can take some curious forms at high altitude. As a 'support climber', I was aware that I was fortunate to have got as far as becoming the Camp 4 Commandant, responsible, in theory, for five face boxes, an equipment dump, nine Sherpas, and a variable number of 'lead climbers' in transit. I became obsessed with actually becoming a Sherpa and increasingly I resented the lead climbers who passed through on oxygen carrying just their personal equipment. I was quite ridiculously touched when, having managed to drag myself and my load up to Camp 5 without oxygen,

Pertemba said, with what I now suspect was heavy sarcasm: 'You are a real Sherpa now.'

Camp 5, perched in its little notch, was filled with slightly unbalanced euphoria. Our Leader, doing his usual thing of shooting up to the front (and rightly so), had now entered his Mad Madhi phase, running out drums of fixed rope in the wrong direction, ranting on at Ang Phurpa about 'really good Sherpa food', working out logistics on his porridge-encrusted electronic calculator, and communicating his befuddled instructions to the outside world on a broken walkie-talkie that had been persuaded to work again by jamming a ballpoint pen into its circuitry.

A few days later I, too, became a transit passenger and moved up to Camp 5 along with Dougal Haston, who was being whisked on oxygen from Camp 2 to Camp 5, like Lenin in his sealed train, to join Doug (who was resting on oxygen) for the first summit attempt. Still playing the Sherpa, I stopped off at the old Camp 4 site and spent a happy couple of hours excavating the Japanese peg-store (we had in fact run out of rock pitons). As I clanked into Camp 5, the triumphant Rock-banders, Nick and Tut, came leaping down the fixed ropes (cries of 'aye, aye, aye . . .' etc.) and there was Doug, the angst-ridden giant, happily sorting out the food and equipment for the summit bid. A changed man, he explained to me that, at the very moment when success was within our grasp, the impossible had happened: the Underground and the Overground had merged into a single upward-thrusting force. Miraculously free, for the moment, of Sandhurst-trained leaders and trades-unionized bureaucrats, at peace with the world, he could direct his all towards what Whillans would call: 'T' job we've come 'ere for.' He was his own man at last.

And he was right about the Leadership: Bonington and his image were now clearly separate, and all the logistics of climbing Everest were condensed into just six heavy loads which just six of us would have to carry through the Rock Band the next day to establish Camp 6. In the jargon of the sociologist, success on Everest requires massive redundancy, duplication and overlap, but this was just what we didn't have. If just one of us didn't make it up the fixed ropes, then the summit bid would be off.

What was more, the route through the Rock Band was not complete nor had a site for Camp 6 been found. Doug and Dougal would have to set off before us, complete the route, fix 300 feet of rope, and find and excavate the site for their Summit Box. In consequence, it was a happy little non-redundant, unduplicated, non-overlapping group that sat enjoying the view and the sunshine that afternoon in the little crow's nest that was Camp 6.

As is the way on such momentous occasions, the conversation was quite spectacularly inane: me getting at the technologically illiterate Dougal, who the evening before had omitted to turn on the oxygen bottle, with the result that we spent the whole night sucking the thin outside air through saliva-filled masks; Mick Burke remarking 'What a lovely spot for a bungalow'; and then Chris, after much deliberation, announcing: 'You know, we must be the highest people on earth.' Since the Americans had just failed on K2, since there was no one on Kanchenjunga, and since we could see that there was no one on Lhotse, I suppose he was right and we *were* the highest people on earth – but not for long! For, as we wished Dougal and Doug good luck and set off down the fixed ropes in the evening sunlight, I knew that for me Everest was over. Still, I consoled myself with the words of the great Maurice Herzog: 'There are other recreational facilities in the lives of men.'*

from *Mountain* (1976)

---

* I quote, of course, from the official translation of *Annapurna*, by P. Boardman, published by The Closed Shop Press, Bradford.

Frederick Burlingham | *An Ordinary Climb*

Now the Aiguille du Moine is an ordinary steep climb on granite. It is not like the Aiguille Verte or the Dent du Géant, where one may expect to be killed.

❈ from *How To Become An Alpinist* (1914)

Janet Adam Smith | The Episode of the Thunderstruck Trousers

Content and exultant, we walked back by the blaeberry path to beer and lemonade at the Montanvert. At dinner we celebrated our best climbing day by ordering something not on the menu. An omelette arrived, so enormous and sustaining that we could hardly face the next course, *tournedos*. Othon, as usual playing the clown after a good day, insisted that the only thing to do with this dish was really to turn your back, and did so, eating off the windowsill, to the scandal of the two Frenchwomen of the blaeberry path – shocked enough anyway by the spectacle of a guide eating with his clients – and to the amusement of the waitresses. Then, over coffee, he unfolded the Episode of the Thunderstruck Trousers. He had arrived one day at the Montanvert from the Col du Géant, soaked through by a thunderstorm; so he had given the girl his coat and breeches to dry. When he went to reclaim them that evening, the girl was full of lamentations and apologies. 'Le pantalon est grillé, m'sieur.' 'Comment, grillé?' 'Oui, m'sieur, il est grillé.' Toasted they were, to that brittle consistency at which cloth needs only one touch to crumble into soot. Very delicately, Othon wore them down to dinner; and then retired stiffly. Next morning he made an early start before anyone could see them. Before long the toasted trousers disintegrated, but no other party saw them until Othon and his client were returning down the Nantillons glacier. A Chamonix man eyed the singed tatters with surprise. 'Lightning on the Grépon,' Othon had glibly explained. 'It struck me on the Râteau de Chèvre, knocked me silly for a second, and left my breeches like this.' Telling the story to us now, he was still surprised at the effect of this happy invention. 'You should have seen his face! And do you

know, there are still people down at Chamonix who believe I
was struck by lightning on the Grépon!'

✻ from *Mountain Holidays* (1946)

III. Offside

Rick Ayres | *Further Notes on Manwatching*

Homo sapiens has many sub-genera, virtually all of which prefer to live in small communities sheltered from the rigours of the climate and gossip columnists' (Homo bill'ickey) eyes, in specially built hives of varying shapes and sizes. In the past year I have concentrated my efforts on spotting and studying three rarer sub-genera of the genus Homo sapiens. I hope that the notes below will greatly assist the manwatcher in studying these delightful if rather coarse creatures.

HOMO ALPINUS

This sub-genus comes in two varieties, (i) the summer alpinus, which likes to sport itself on steep cliffs that receive a lot of sunshine, and (ii) the winter alpinus, which is only found in areas with an arctic-type climate. Both species are rarely found below 2,000 feet in the lands near the poles and 4-5,000 feet in the lands nearer the equator.

Markings – in the early morning and late afternoon or all day, if the sun does not shine, bulky, gaudy and brightly coloured skins are sported. In warm conditions this layer is shed; a rough, ill-fitting, thin hairy layer, which can be brightly coloured but more usually is stained and soiled, can then be seen. In bright sunlight, dark patches develop which protect the eyes. This species also sports a hump on the back: the Homo alpinus britannicus sports a very large and heavy hump.

Warning – The winter alpinus has retractable claws and spikes primarily for use when climbing snow and ice. I would advise all watchers to keep at a respectable distance.

Movements and displays – the Homo alpinus usually moves with a certain grace early in the day, walking with a light springy step. This soon disappears, especially if he is struggling through deep soft snow (Homo eskimos have solved this problem) or is walking uphill for a great length of time. Homo plancus has solved this problem. There appears to be some interaction between the plancus and Homo alpinus. However, some of the latter regard the former in the same way as Homo pouftus. The summer alpinus can exhibit a rather fine series of spider and crab-like movements on steep rock: these can be a joy to watch.

Calls – a series of gasping and panting noises when walking upwards or through steep snow. When falling, surprised yelps may be heard and on reaching the maximum height attainable, a varied selection of yells, grunts, pantings and hoarse whispers.

Numbers – occasionally found individually but more usually in pairs or multiples of two. It is possible to see a large number on the same route at the same time. If this is the case, look out for the quaint habits of the Homo alpinus continentalus, namely his ceremonial stone throwing if another party is below him or pulling on the gossamer thread of the party in front.

HOMO CRUSTACEOUS

This is a migrant that, with patience, can be found in any spot winter or summer. He will spend the night in a small shelter that he carries on his back. This sub-genus is an animal that prefers isolation, therefore he is usually found alone or with his dog (chasing sheep) or with one partner of the same species (possibly the opposite sex). On one occasion I was lucky enough to see ten all under the same shelter – it was a very wet night.

Markings – usually a green or an orange outer shell with a less gaudy and bulky skin underneath. Homo crustaceous has a well-developed hump of many compartments on his back, usually only marginally smaller than that carried by Homo alpinus britannicus.

Movements and display – a vigorous and exciting display can be observed at dusk as the animal prepares to sleep. Firstly, he checks that his nest is as he would like it to be, then getting on to all fours he backs into the shelter taking off his protective skins as he goes: at the same time he is always on the look-out for intruders. Eventually, when half in his cocoon, he turns

about and lies on his back. Here the thrashing and wiggling associated with this creature begins, a display enhanced by the enclosed nature of the shelter, and so he sleeps, exhausted.

The Homo crustaceous has a rather unusual night ritual. Usually at around 3 o'clock in the morning or just after it starts raining, a preliminary warning is given to possible intruders by a shaking, fumbling and finally a tearing of the shelter fabric. The animal emerges from its sleeping cocoon in a drowsy and belligerent state. A short distance from the shelter he begins to urinate. The reason for doing this is obscure but it is probably used to stake out his territory.

Mating rituals – this is the only animal out of the three sub-genera described here that I have seen mating – it is an unusual affair. Firstly the female enters the shelter and enters her sleeping cocoon; this is quite a lengthy process. The male meanwhile paces up and down outside the shelter and appears to make encouraging and reassuring noises. Eventually he is allowed to make an inspection of the nest, checking that it is set out properly. To show his respect and trust for the female he now leaves the nest and enters it again backwards, on all fours. The cocoon-entering display takes place along with many soft calls and whispers. At this stage the portable light source is extinguished so further visual details cannot be given. The ritual continues with billowings and stretching of the shelter fabric along with groaning, coos, moaning and slapping noises. After a relatively quiet period a frenzied exit by both sexes from the sleeping cocoons is made. The cooing and groaning noises start again and after a while subside to nothing. All that remains is the ceremonial re-entering of the sleeping cocoons.

Calls – the Homo crustaceous is a quiet animal and is rarely heard. However, both behaviour and calls can be extremely aggressive when passing through peat bogs and newly planted coniferous plantations.

HOMO VERTICALUS

A summer migrant that is only found in areas with a favourable climate, many beer halls and steep cliffs. On occasions, this sub-genus can be observed in the habitat favoured by the Homo alpinus.

The Homo verticalus can be seen alone but they usually pair off for the day, although sometimes as many as five or six can be seen together at one time. Usually these animals all have the same coloured skins with numerals on the back. Many pairs can be seen congregating in relative harmony on cliffs near roads and beer halls.

Markings – this animal is commonly observed wearing only a thin skin in various shades of blue and brown, normally badly worn, stained and soiled. If the Homo verticalus occurs in pairs or more, then a thin, brightly coloured gossamer thread joins each one to another. Shorter but more brightly coloured strands encircle the neck and hang from the waist. It is normally the uppermost animal who has most of these.

Calls – a series of hoarse and coarse yelps. Cries that indicate surprise can be heard when one falls off. Other animals of the same genus usually erupt into a varied response of jeers, whistling, catcalls and laughing on these occasions. Homo grokkus, if watching, usually gasps and stares fixated.

Displays – these are varied and can be similar to those of Homo alpinus. The movements on the cliffs can be graceful and athletic. However, Homo verticalus incompetus finds many types of movements impossible and appears to walk from one cliff to the next with a ritual head-shaking and muttering.

HOW TO ATTRACT THESE ANIMALS INTO YOUR GARDEN

A large rockery, which will have to consist of several summits most of which have precipitous faces and connecting ridges, will have to be made. This alone will please the summer alpinus and Homo verticalus. Waterfalls, snowfields, cornices and a refrigeration unit will be required to attract the winter alpinus.

If you wish to attract the Homo verticalus only, then a small rockery consisting of many small precipitous faces along with many roads, tracks and beer holes must be made.

The Homo crustaceous is a much more difficult animal to attract; only those with very large gardens will succeed. Many Monroes, tops and summits will have to be built, interspersed with deep valleys, small water-courses and small grass patches so that this animal can construct his shelter in complete isolation.

ARE THEY GREGARIOUS?

Great care will be needed in selecting other sub-genera of Homo sapiens that will be compatible with those described above. Difficulties will arise on the social scene because the alpinus, crustaceous and verticalus have an affliction, similar to the plancus, of talking non-stop about their respective activities, boring the pants off any other sub-genera. These animals, however, seem to have a good working relationship with Homo agriculturus. Do not be misguided enough to hope for the same relationship with the Homo nature conservancy apus and the Homo forestry commission illegitimus. Such a combination will usually end up in a pitched battle. If this is the case the only form of action that it is safe to take is to introduce Homo BMC quangous that will intervene and draw up access notices that will hopefully restore peace.

At present I have no notes on the mating rituals of Homo alpinus and Homo verticalus. If any manwatcher can provide me with details I would be extremely grateful.

�֍ from *Climber and Rambler* (1981)

J. W. Muller | *Survivors*

Geology consists of stones and dirt . . . The large stones are known as mountains. Mountains are of little value, being exceedingly primitive and rudely built. Their chief use is for climbing. The only practical result from climbing a mountain is to climb down again. Naturers who climb mountains for sport are known as mountaineers. Those who descend are known as survivors. There also are professional survivors known as guides.

❈ from *First Aid to Naturers* (1913)

Rex Slim | The Gearfreak Caper

EDITOR'S NOTE Rex Slim is a pen-name adopted by Guy Waterman for this piece of hokum. Avid followers of detective fiction will immediately recognize the obvious derivation.

In my business you got to be able to spot a mealticket from a dry hole right off. I was pretty sure Lady Luck had sent me home a winner when this tweedy gent with the pipe comes through the door marked CLAUDIUS FOX PRIVATE INVESTIGATOR and walks up to my desk.

He smelled like money. Trouble too. But that's my bag, isn't it?

'Mr Fox?' he queried.

'That's what the name says on the door,' I countered.

His suit was rumpled and not exactly new, but you could tell he didn't get it off the rack at Burtons. His shirt was expensive and the tie was as conservative as a baked potato. But what caught my eye was the tie clasp: a thin, small, neatly embossed golden dollar-sign. I liked that.

'My name's Godfrey Gearfreak. I need help and I'm willing to pay for it,' he started in, me not objecting to that last part.

'I've never dealt with a private detective before, but I don't want this to get to the police. You see,' his eyes fell, 'I'm being blackmailed.'

I'd heard this story before. Only this one turned out to have a new wrinkle.

I motioned him to a chair and drew paper and pencil from under the flask in the desk drawer. 'Tell me all about it,' I mused in my most understanding tone.

'My wife and I used to go rock climbing together a lot. We met in an Alpine Club beginners' group. We used to go to Den Lane, Brownstones, vacations in the Tetons, Chamonix, Zermatt, everywhere together.'

'Sounds nice and healthy,' I smiled. 'What went wrong?'

He plunged in: 'The equipment – all the climbing gear; I found it fascinating; she was bored by it. I got all the latest catalogues – Chouinard, Moac, Troll, you name it. I grooved on the Mountain Safety Research Newsletters. I had to try all the latest hardware, each new belay plate and seat harness, not to mention all the new tent designs, pack frames, sleeping bags, stoves . . .'

'And your wife didn't like your spending the money?' I put in.

'It's not that. We can afford that kind of money.' I liked to hear him say that; it gave me a warm feeling in my wallet.

His voice lowered. 'She just never took an interest in the equipment. She still wants to go hiking and climbing on weekends. Scrambling around on the rocks is all right, I suppose, but there's so much new gear to try out and read about, I don't want to waste all my free time just out there climbing around.

'Christ, Claudius,' he blurted, 'who wants to sweat out some lousy VS move when you could be looking at and talking about this hot new foamback material for cagoules that uses a super K-coated nylon taffeta with a .050-inch layer of bonded foam and a lining of thin nylon tricot?'

No question, I had to agree with Gearfreak there.

'Well, I found out there's a place in this town where they'll set you up with a girl who knows all about climbing equipment and will talk with you for an hour about any gear you want to talk about – for a price.'

He paused, embarrassed. 'Go on,' I urged.

'I never wanted to get involved. I'm just looking for a quick stimulating exchange of ideas on all the latest gear – then I want the girl to leave.

'They've got all kinds of girls – some of them know all the latest tents, some can tell you about ropes and their test strength, some are technical ice-climbing specialists.' He sighed a crooked, bitter sigh: 'It's really satisfying, Claudius, to spend an evening secluded with a girl who really *understands* how baffles are superior to sewn-through seams, and can talk intelligently and sympathetically about proper stitching, who appreciates the difference between goose down and duck down, and who isn't afraid to talk openly about foam as a medium for sleeping bags.'

'All sounds great,' I commented. 'What's the prob?'

'Blackmail! I've been arranging these rendezvous for several months. The price was stiff, but it was worth it. Now they're upping the ante – asking for real money – or they tell my wife.'

His voice dropped to a whisper: 'They've even got a photo of me showing a Sticht belay plate to a young girl in lederhosen.'

I was intrigued. I'd heard that the boys down at the Vice Squad were working on some big-time racket involving outdoorsy-types, but I also knew they weren't getting anywhere on the case. Maybe this was a lead.

'Tell me what you know about this operation,' I hunched over the pad.

He demurred. 'But will you help me? Will you take the case?'

I looked again at that thin, small, neatly embossed golden dollar-sign tie clasp. 'Seventy-five pounds a day plus expenses. And I don't guarantee results. But I've got some hunches I'd like to play.'

He looked assured. I had me a client.

After he left, I also had me a packet more of notes on all he knew, including the telephone number of his contact. I was ready to make my first move.

Going out to a pay phone so it could not be traced, I plugged in my pennies and dialled the seven delectable digits. A husky voice like Harlow with bronchitis answered.

I started off briskly: 'I understand a fellow could get a little companionable talk on the advantages and disadvantages of different lightweight stoves at this party.'

'I'm totally mystified as to what you're talking about, mister,' responded the decidedly unmystified voice.

'I have a hundred here to refresh your memory,' I growled.

Madam husky-voice was suddenly all business. 'Do you want to talk heating capacity or weight-and-volume, honey?'

'The works.' I thought it best not to seem cheap.

'That C-note will get you a nice evening with a girl who knows all the stoves and has tried them out in high winds and at different altitudes. She was one of the first to use the Globetrotter.'

'Sounds like my ticket,' I opined, gave a room number at the Belmont and hung up.

An hour later I answered the buzzer at this same room number to see a shapely young sheba who was all Miss Outdoors from the tip of her balaclava right down to the toes of her Civettas. In between she filled out her climbing breeches and L. L. Bean sweater like so many well-filled (but just right) stuff sacks.

Her Karrimor bulged with odd shapes and sizes of stoves.

'Hi, I'm Bobbi,' she cooed sweetly.

'Baby, I don't know how you got by the house dick,' I winced as I pulled her into the room. 'Anyone can tell you're an equipment nut.'

'A five-spot usually keeps them happy,' she smiled confidently. Unshouldering her rucksack, she shot a glance around the room. 'Would you like to begin by comparing the heating properties of the Optimus IIIB with the newer Globetrotter?'

I parried: 'I've heard that the Globetrotter's a fabulous heating machine, but won't simmer on low heat like the Optimus.' I had to string her along, see what she'd do, see how far she'd go.

'True.' She laughed a hollow, brittle laugh. 'But the weight of that old IIIB never appealed to me. And since you have to carry a fuel bottle anyway . . .'

She started in and kept it up, with just an occasional query or rebuttal from me, for fully an hour. Here she was, probably not old enough to buy a set-up in a Brauhaus, but she had all the hardened flippance of the jaded equipment freak. I was amazed. I mean, I've been around, but this was something new.

When she got through explaining how the adaptor valves for the new Rich-Moor stoves accommodated several varieties of fuel, I got up, stretched, and taking two fifties out of my wallet, stuffed them in the outside pocket of her rucksack.

'Say, you're nice,' she grinned suddenly. 'Would you like to do it again some time? Or maybe try something a little different . . . a little unusual?'

'What'd you have in mind?' I countered.

'Well, I have a girl friend you'd like,' she purred. 'The two of us could come up and talk about cross-country ski wax for a really divine evening. We could even get into . . .' her voice trailed off, but her lips shaped the word, '. . . bindings . . .' She winked.

'I think we might make a deal,' I murmured, bluffing. 'I'll call you in a day or so', and I ushered her and her rucksack out the door, familiarly patting her D-rings as she passed.

Pay dirt! I knew I had stumbled right into just the mess the Vice Squad was after. I suppressed a snicker. I knew the lieutenant would be climbing walls when he found I had beaten him to the quarry again.

Before I took the direct route to my prey, though, I thought I ought to do a little advance nosing around through a third party, a certain shady character of my acquaintance, name of Slightly Roddey, who is willing to give me underworld information on occasion in exchange for my *not* giving the boys downtown certain information about Slightly Roddey.

Slightly was his usual obnoxious and uncooperative self until reminded of the advantages of being on this side of those Parkhurst walls.

'The Vice boys haven't got to first base on this one,' Slightly told me over a draft in the Shady Deal Café down on Lower Filth Street.

'This operation is really big-time and the cover's held up airtight so far.

'For fifty bills you can spend a couple of hours with a brunette going over the pros and cons of A-frame tents versus the exoskeleton design, reviewing ventilation condensation, tunnel entrances, mosquito netting, zippers and cookstove holes.

'For just twenty-five, you can get a set-up with a leggy Swedish broad, lighting lanterns and stoves and testing for beryllium and carbon monoxide.

'If you're into technical climbing, you can climb into and out of every seat harness, chest harness, and leg loop in the book with two cuties who can tell you the fall force which each one could absorb and will listen sympathetically to all you want to tell them about different hard hats, even including their energy absorption and lateral rigidity. That would cost you seventy-five quid.'

Slightly paused to order another brew.

'Write down this name: Gloria Rucksack. She's the brains *and* the muscle behind this one, from what I hear.'

'What's her background?' I wheedled.

'She's an equipment nut from way back. You know the Berghaus fancy warmlite tent?'

'The one with the unique condensation-dispelling properties?' I questioned.

'That's the one. Well, Berghaus don't know it, but Gloria Rucksack spent a weekend in the pilot model before they did.'

I gulped.

'You know Dirty Harry's new sleeping bags at Alpine Designs?' went on Slightly. 'She slept in it the first night the baffles were stitched.'

'With or without Dirty Harry?' I quipped.

'You want solid info or witty repartee?' Slightly shot back. 'She knows them all – Davies, Fisher, the Brigham brothers. Anyway, the place you want is a little backpacking supply store on the outskirts of town, Northern Alpine Sports. It's a front, of course. The real operation runs out of the back of the store. You'd probably find Gloria there.'

An hour later, when I walked into Northern Alpine Sports, a young man in vibrams asked if he could help me.

'I'd like to see a rucksack,' I croaked.

'For what purpose?' he inquired.

'Glory-a only knows,' I muttered.

'In that case, go right on back,' he knowingly waved down a long hall that led to a door marked STOCK ROOM EMPLOY-EES ONLY. I pushed open the door and gingerly stepped in.

Here indeed was Gloria Rucksack's pleasure palace. The place was a perfect set-up. A huge high-ceilinged room, with windows along one side as tall as your grandmother's giraffe. Only no light showed through the heavy maroon velvet floor-to-tall-ceiling curtains, embroidered with thick gold sash. The light was supplied by three glittering silver chandeliers suspended from the ornate ceiling. An oriental carpet large enough to fly in Farouk and all his concubines buried the floor. Victorian decor all the way.

And girls? Wow! A trio of beauties sat on one outsized sofa, provocatively leafing through pages of Pindisports catalogues. A gorgeous redhead in matching crimson breeches, who looked like she'd just been poured into her Whillans seat harness like thick strawberry jam, was sorting hexentrics voluptuously on the floor at one end. Slouched in an armchair near the door, a slender pretty girl no more than seventeen years old was opening and closing Jumars and Gibbs ascenders.

Within seconds after I entered, a slinky black girl sidled up to me from nowhere, slipping her slim hips in and out of a wrap-around pack frame, and breathed huskily: 'Would you like to go upstairs and talk about different kinds of back bands?'

'Catch you later at Camp Four, baby,' I snapped out of the corner of my mouth. 'I got other things on my mind right now.'

A honey blonde in a leopard-skin 60/40 whispered at me from the other side. 'If you're into technical ice, we could have a cosy chat about the test strengths of Salewa tubulars versus wart hogs. And I have a new wrinkle on how to use a Terrordactyl that would tickle you.'

Before I could answer, a familiar husky tone from behind me intervened: 'Later, Birgit. This one's for me.'

Swinging round, I saw before me the queen mama of them all – a statuesque raven-haired venus who would make anyone forget to button down his super-gaiters. Her skirt was like a good tent fly – form-fitted and not too long. And the blouse material was strictly sewn-through.

'You look like you could use a sociable brew in the back room, honey,' she purred and guided me toward a low door near the back, just past a wrought-ebony bookcase sporting titles like *Freedom of the Hills*, *Advanced Rockcraft*, early Chouinard catalogues, and a handsome leatherbound complete set of *Climber and Rambler*.

She slipped a key chain out of her bosom and sorted through the Swiss Army knife, Taylor pocket altimeter and Dwyer wind meter until she came to a tiny key for the little door. But not before I noticed on that key chain one other little trinket . . . a thin, small, neatly embossed golden dollar-sign.

I followed her into a richly appointed little boudoir and as she walked ahead of me, I said: 'Nice little pad you have here, Gloria Rucksack – or should I say . . . Mrs Gearfreak!'

She wheeled around sporting a new piece of equipment – a shiny little black revolver that I knew she didn't pick up at Brigham's. 'That's right, Fox, you walked yourself right into the middle of more than you bargained for this time.'

'I don't get it, baby,' I sauntered, stalling, trying to look calm. 'Your old man said he couldn't get you to talk about clevis pins at breakfast.'

'That creep?' she snarled. 'He doesn't know his rear end from a cookstove hole. What he doesn't know about equipment would fill three Karrimor catalogues. Just as soon as I get this operation a little more profitable, it'll be Good-bye Godfrey! And meanwhile, Foxie, you're going to take a little hike of your own – down the middle of the river in a pair of cement P As.'

I thought fast – and acted faster. With one swift karate chop, I separated Miss Glorialocks from her shiny black plaything and in another motion swooped an extra large down mummy bag over her head. She ripped out her Swiss Army knife and cut her way out, filling the room with more feathers than you'll see at a Northern Goose Hoedown on Hudson Bay. By this time, though, Your Humble Narrator had the revolver and the outing was over.

The rest of the story came out downtown, and today Miss Rucksack – Mrs Gearfreak – is doing a ten-year bivouac in a really windproof stand-up tent at Holloway.

Except for my cheque from Mr Godfrey Gearfreak in the mail, I neither saw nor heard from him again. But I've been told that he now roams the Pennines, with no climbing hardware, no tent, and just an old army blanket for nights, in which he rolls all his simple belongings, so that he needs no fancy pack. They say he takes no interest in the latest gadgets and gear of the other climbers or hikers he meets on the trail, but simply invites them to join him in looking at the birds and the wild flowers.

❅ from *Off Belay* (1976)

S. Russell Jones | Mission Aborted

'Here's a message. It's urgent,' said Jones on the phone.
'There's a fool lost on Snowdon. He went off alone
With the wind coming up and the glass going down,
So he's missing this evening through acting the clown.'
'We need speed,' said the Leader and started to shout.
'We are leaving. Get weaving, for all must turn out.
Check your compasses, anoraks, Karrimor Sacs
And emergency packs on the Land Rover racks.
Get the stretchers collected. We must make a start
If we want to be searching by first sparrow-fart.
See you butter some butties and brew up some chai,
With a wee drop of rum in the Thermos for Dai,
For we'll get in a sweat, then be frozen and wet;
And before you forget see you net in the Set.'
Then the Driver came running, adjusting his flies,
And the Leader said 'Sidney, a word to the wise.
We are clear of the town, so just keep your foot down
If the crown of the road shows no white on the brown.
But there's ice on the edges and frost on the grass,
And we'll run into snow when we get to the Pass.'
They went slow on the snow, but it just put the lid
On their chances when Sid hit the ditch in a skid,
For a ditch is all right on a warm summer night
For a kiss with a miss who is blissfully tight.
But a ditch is a bitch when you pitch off the track
Into four feet of slush with the wheels sliding back.
Then the Driver was waving his arms in despair
Like the prop of a 'copter that's chopping the air,
While his Mate lost his plate so could not clench his teeth
As the icy-cold water came up from beneath,
And the Leader emerged with a bump on his head.
'You have buckled the bumper, you bugger,' he said,

And so man after man waded out of the mud,
And some spat out a curse but no worse and no blood.
Then came Rhys the Police and old Ianto the Slate,
Who said 'Some silly sod must have smashed through my
gate.'
P.C. Hughes brought the news that ignited a fuse
For explosions of swearing and filthy abuse,
For no climber was missing. The tale was all wrong
And the 'climber' found singing a scandalous song
About Wales and its ales and the frails he'd enjoyed
As he toyed with a barmaid in Betws-y-Coed.

from *Climber and Rambler* (1981)

H. W. Tilman | The Abominable Snowman

I have here collected and commented upon all the available evidence supporting or denying the existence of this creature. I do not claim to be *the* authority (I know of no one who does), but I happen to have some first-hand knowledge and I have read everything that has been written about it. I shall perhaps be criticized for treating a serious inquiry in a light-hearted way, but it is possible to be serious without being dull. 'Nothing like a little judicious levity', as Michael Finsbury remarked.

Most of the published evidence has appeared not in scientific journals but on the leader page of a respectable daily to which even its enemies will not deny probity and a sense of tradition. Indeed, all who share and respect this last quality must have noticed with regret how the hospitality of those venerable columns was abused by the iconoclasts in a determined attack upon the 'Abominable Snowman', denying its existence or that it ever had existed. No great harm, however, was done. Bear tracks in the course of a column and a half were shown to have been made by bears; wolves, otters and hares were found to make tracks after their kind, and when the dust of conflict had settled the 'Abominable Snowman' survived to pursue his evasive, mysterious, terrifying existence, unruffled as the snow he treads, unmoved as the mountains in which he dwells, uncaught, unspecified, but not unhonoured. But I anticipate.

All those interested in the Himalaya and mountain exploration generally are indebted to the first Mount Everest expedition, the reconnaissance of 1921, on many counts; not least because it is to them we owe the introduction of the 'Abominable Snowman' to mountaineering and scientific circles. It is very fitting that a mountain which was for long itself mysterious, whose summit is still untrod, and which has been the scene of many strange happenings, should be the starting-point for an inquiry of this nature. The leader of that expedition, Col. Howard Bury, came across footprints resembling those of a human being on the Lhakpa La, the 21,000-foot pass north-east of the mountain. In an article which he telegraphed home he referred to this and to the assertion of his porters that they were the tracks of 'the Wild Men of the Snows'. As a safeguard, and in order to dissociate himself from such an extravagant and laughable belief, he put no less than three exclamation marks after the statement; but the telegraph system makes no allowance for subtleties and the finer points of literature, the saving signs were omitted, and the news was accorded very full value at home.

Thus the prodigy was born though not yet properly christened; but a godfather was at hand at Darjeeling in the form of a Mr Henry Newman. Mr Newman got into conversation with some of these Everest porters on their return to Darjeeling and obtained a full description of the 'Wild Men' – how their feet were *turned backward to enable them to climb easily,** and how their hair was so long and matted that when going downhill it fell over their eyes. The name they applied to them was 'Metch kangmi' – 'kangmi' meaning 'snowman', and the word 'metch' Mr Newman translated as 'abominable'. As he wrote long after in a letter to *The Times*: 'The whole story seemed such a joyous creation I sent it to one *or two newspapers.*† Later I was told by a Tibetan expert that I had not quite got the force of the word "metch" which did not mean "abominable" quite so much as filthy or disgusting, somebody wearing filthy tattered clothing. The Tibetan word means something like that but is much more emphatic, just as a Tibetan is more dirty than anyone else.' Mr Newman then offered his explanation of the 'Metch kangmi': 'This, I am convinced, is that in Tibet there is no capital punishment, and that men guilty of grave crimes are simply turned out of their villages or monastery. They live in caves like wild animals, and in order to obtain food become expert thieves and robbers. Also in parts of Tibet and the Himalaya many caves are inhabited by ascetics and others striving to

* This is interesting because the same backwards technique is sometimes adopted by climbers wearing crampons (ice-claws) when climbing very steep ice or snow slopes.

† This may have accounted for the stir caused by Col. Howard Bury's laconic statement.

obtain magical powers by cutting themselves off from mankind and refusing to wash.'

Here then we have the explanation of how the 'Snowman' acquired his eponymous title and a plausible suggestion as to his reality. For my part I cannot accept such a solution for the problem of tracks I myself have seen or for some of those reported by other travellers which we shall have to discuss presently. We mountaineers may be wrong in thinking that a liking for the high snows is peculiar to us, but I should be astonished to find a native, Tibetan or any other, however guilty, ascetic, or careless about washing, who shared our taste for such places. There are ascetics to be found living not far below the snout of the Rongbuk glacier, but they remain immured in their caves, tended by their admirers, and never in my experience mortify the flesh still further by a promenade up the glacier. In the desire to keep this appendix as short as possible I have selected very rigorously from the large number of letters available, and I notice one from Capt. Henniker, RE, more for the sake of the charm of the anecdote than for its relevance. The letter from Capt. Henniker (now, I think, Lt-Col. Henniker, DSO) supported this new theory of Mr Newman's with an actual example, but I cannot accept it as in any way invalidating the refutation of it which I have just given, for a 17,000-foot pass on a well-known route in Ladakh is not on all fours with the places where strange tracks have been observed, such as the Snow Lake or the Zemu Gap, both of which are extremely remote from human habitations of any kind or known routes. In 1930 on the summit of a 17,000-foot pass in Ladakh, Capt. Henniker met a man completely naked except for a loin cloth. It was bitterly cold and snowing gently. When he expressed some natural astonishment he met with the reply given in perfect English: 'Good morning, Sir, and a Happy Christmas to you' (it was actually July). The hardy traveller was an MA of an English University (Cambridge, one suspects) and was on a pilgrimage for the good of his soul. He explained that one soon got used to the cold and that many Hindus did the same thing.

It will be seen after reviewing the evidence which I shall marshal for and against the existence of the 'Snowman' that

'Good morning, sir, and a Happy Christmas.'

except for one instance of small value everything turns upon the interpretation of footprints. And if fingerprints can hang a man, as they frequently do, surely footprints may be allowed to establish the existence of one. I agree that for some of the many strange tracks which have been reported there is either a definite or a probable explanation, but for others there is not. Not unnaturally the 'Abominable Snowman' always leaves his tell-tale prints in snow, which, for obvious reasons, is an unsatisfactory medium. The identification of a photograph of a footprint in snow, taken after the lapse of an unknown number of hours or days after it was made, is no easy matter, and while I do not question the interpretation of the experts I marvel at their confidence. It is true, and it is a pity, that no European has seen or even thinks he has seen an 'Abominable Snowman', but such negative evidence is not really of great value because the number of Europeans who visit his haunts in the course of a year could probably be counted on the fingers of one hand. On the contrary there are many Tibetans and other dwellers near the Himalaya who do claim to have seen him, and we Europeans, I hope, are not to arrogate to ourselves a monopoly of truth. Due weight, too, must be accorded to a tradition which is so very widespread, which covers most of the Himalayan regions from the Karakoram in the west to as far east as the Upper Salween.

Before marshalling the main evidence I must deal briefly with the solitary exception noticed above. In a letter, a Mr H. B. Hudson recounted an experience he had when camping in the Pir Panjal in a glade of pines at about 8,000 feet. 'It was towards evening', he wrote, 'and my servants, all devout Musulmans, were cooking. All of a sudden there was a ghastly yell from among the trees not far away. My servants were obviously terrified as I asked what had made that hideous noise. We sat round the fire discussing what I shall now explain very briefly.' There is no call to follow Mr Hudson's brief explanation for it is merely a recapitulation of native beliefs – Rishis masquerading as bears, spirits of women who have died in childbirth or of persons who have died violent deaths, lonely and longing for human companionship. What a pity Mr Hudson did not take active steps to investigate that 'ghastly yell' instead of posing questions for the Society for Psychical Research. We might have learnt something interesting, although in the terrain he describes – pine trees and a mere 8,000 feet – I fear it would not have been anything germane to this inquiry. Himalayan travellers are constantly hearing weird noises in far more likely terrain, all of which may safely be attributed to the forces of nature acting on ice, snow and rock.

After the instance of 1921 from the region of Mount Everest the first reliable report of strange footprints came from the well-known traveller Mr Ronald Kaulback. Writing about a journey to the Upper Salween in 1936 he reported having seen, at a height of 16,000 feet, 'five sets of tracks which looked exactly as though made by a bare-footed man'. Two of his porters thought they were the tracks of snow leopard, two thought they were those of 'mountain men' which they described as like a man, white-skinned, with long hair on head, arms and shoulders. Mr Kaulback added that in those parts there were *no bears*. Corroborative evidence was tendered by Wing-Comdr Beauman who had seen similar tracks near the source of the Ganges in Garhwal in the Central Himalaya. Various correspondents offered explanations for these tracks, in particular experts from the Natural History Museum. First, they were said to be those of large langur monkeys, large heavily built animals, whose footprints would be little smaller than those of a man. It is not their custom to walk on their hind legs and they are arboreal in their habits, but it was suggested they might traverse the open between one forest and another. To this it was objected that the tracks were seen 3,000 feet above the tree line, and that although he had spent five months there Mr Kaulback had neither seen nor heard of any monkeys.

The experts withdrew their langur from the competition, the shoe not fitting, and produced their Cinderella: 'We are told there are no bears', they countered, 'but what of the Giant Panda or Snow Bear? Is it not possible the tracks were made by an unknown relative of this species?' The last suggestion was considered a shrewd one by Mr Kaulback, who wrote to say he was ashamed he had not thought of it himself. Possibly there was a hint of sarcasm in this admission, since he added a rider to the effect that he had seen no panda-like skins or even heard of such animals in those parts, nor were there any bamboo shoots, a *sine qua non* for pandas without which they languish and die.

So far then we have as candidates for the authorship of queer tracks, seen on three several occasions, snow leopards, outlaws, bears, pandas, ascetics, langurs, or x the unknown quantity (which we may as well call the 'Abominable Snowman'), roughly in that order of probability. This was the uncertain state of the poll in the summer of 1937, but in the autumn of that year a new and important witness appeared who in one stroke settled or was thought to have settled the matter out of hand. The bear was declared the winner and our 'Abominable' friend was found to be not only at the bottom of the poll but a complete impostor who should never have stood and who must forfeit his deposit.

The evidence which was thought conclusive by himself and others came from Mr F. S. Smythe. In the summer of that year, on a snow pass 16,500 feet high in the Central Himalaya, Mr Smythe and his Sherpa porters found 'the imprints of a huge foot, apparently of a biped'. Without any ado the Sherpas declared they were those of a 'mirka' or Snowman, but Mr Smythe, with small respect for tradition and less for his Sherpas' zoology, set himself to measuring and photographing the tracks with the calm scientific diligence of a Sherlock Holmes or Dr Thorndike's gifted assistant. So convinced were the three Sherpas that they volunteered a written statement which I quote in full because it is upon this weak hook that Mr Smythe hangs his innocent victim: 'We, Wangdi Nurbu, Nurbu Bhotia, and Pasang Urgen, were accompanying Mr Smythe over a pass when we saw tracks which we *know* to be those of a "mirka" or "wild man". We have often seen bear, snow leopard, and other animal tracks, but we swear that these tracks were none of these. We have never seen a "mirka" because anyone who sees one dies or is killed, but there are pictures of the tracks which are the same as we have seen in Tibetan monasteries.'

To identify the footprints of a thing one has never seen by a picture of what a Tibetan monk imagines it to be is a fairly bold proceeding. Fear sometimes makes men bold and these Sherpas were frightened men who, having jumped to an erroneous conclusion, felt obliged to stick to it to palliate their fear. Hence their statement and the wild remark about Tibetan pictures to support it. As anyone who has seen a 'thang-ka' will allow, Tibetan painting is decidedly post-impressionist. One would as soon expect to find in a monastery an accurate drawing of a battleship as of a 'mirka's' foot.

Mr Smythe's photos were duly developed, as he assured us, 'under conditions that precluded any subsequent faking'; but he need not have bothered, it is not his facts which are suspect but his inferences. The prints were submitted to the Zoological pundits, headed by Dr Julian Huxley, and were by them pronounced (not without some scientific snarling) to be those of a bear, *Ursus arctus pruinosus*. Whereupon Mr Smythe, triumphantly flourishing his Sherpas' affidavit, announced to his expectant audience that 'the tracks described in recent letters to *The Times* were made by this bear, and that a superstition of the Himalaya is now explained, at all events to Europeans'. In short, *delenda est homo niveus disgustans*; moreover, any tracks seen in the snow in the past, the present, or the future may safely be ascribed to bears. As a *non-sequitur* this bears comparison with the classic example: 'No wonder they call this place Stony Stratford, I was never so bitten by fleas in all my life.'

Had it not so happened that the season of 1937 was a very active one in the Himalaya the Snowman's case might well have gone by default. Stunned by Mr Smythe's authority few paused to reflect that this apparently fatal blow was merely a matter of three frightened Sherpas making a mistake over some obvious bear tracks, and they meekly accepted his assertion for proof. However, the friends of fair play and seemingly lost causes were comforted to see this assertion immediately challenged by one who had just returned from the Himalaya who wrote under the rather unnecessary pseudonym of 'Bhalu'. In the course of an expedition to the Karakoram, while traversing the upper basin of the Biafu glacier (Sir Martin Conway's 'Snow Lake'), he and two Sherpas had seen tracks which, whatever else they might be, were certainly not those of bear. 'They were roughly circular', he wrote, 'about a foot in diameter, 9 in. deep, and 18 in. apart. They lay in a straight line without any right or left stagger, nor was there any sign of overlap as would be the case with a four-footed beast. The Sherpas diagnosed them as those of a Snow-man ("yeti" was their term) and they thought he was the smaller man-eating variety and not his larger yak-eating brother. When I pointed out that no one had been in those parts for 30 years and that he must be devilish hungry they were not amused. I was short of film but considering the subject and the suspicious nature of scientists I thought I could spare one. In fact I made two exposures but being less skilful than Mr Smythe made both on the same negative. A few days later in another glacier valley, bear tracks were everywhere and were quickly recognized as such by the Sherpas and myself. They were no more like the others than those of a two-toed ant-eater.'

'Bhalu's' blundering stupidity with his camera cannot be too much deplored, especially when we consider Mr Smythe's cool, efficient handling of a similar discovery. In default of a photo of the tracks he produced a sketch which roused the naturalists to start a fresh hare, or rather otter. One wrote suggesting that the tracks were those of an otter progressing in a series of leaps. 'The Indian otter (*Lutra lutra nair*)', he wrote, 'has already been reported from high altitudes in the Himalaya.' This hint was snapped up by one brother naturalist who endorsed it and added that he had used it himself some years before to dispose of the Loch Ness Monster; and it was snapped at by another who unkindly pointed out that the otter in question was *monticola* not *nair*, the former being found in the Himalaya, the latter only in Southern India and Ceylon.

Amidst the snarls of the zoologists it was pleasing to hear a modest pipe from one signing himself 'Foreign Sportsman' (strange pseudonym) who introduced yet another small piece of first-hand evidence. He wrote: 'Bhalu's contribution to the discussion was welcome. His spirited defence of the Abominable Snowman wilting under the combined attack of Mr Smythe and the Zoological Society reminded me of Kipling's lines:

> Horrible, hairy, human, with paws like hands in prayer,
> Making his supplication rose Adam-Zad the Bear.

The burden of proof has now been shifted to the shoulders of the Society who must now find us a one-legged, carnivorous bird, weighing several hundredweight. While not wishing to draw a red herring across this fresh line of inquiry may I recount an experience of my own in Garhwal last year. With two Sherpas I was crossing the Bireh Ganga glacier when we came upon tracks made in crisp snow which resembled nothing so much as those of an elephant. I have followed elephant spoor often and could have sworn we were following one then but for the comparative scarcity of those beasts in the Central Himalaya. 'Pshaw! A falling boulder!' I hear some grizzled Himalayan veteran exclaim. True, in certain conditions boulders can and do make a remarkably regular series of indentations like tracks, but I have yet to see a boulder of its own volition hop for a mile over an almost flat glacier.'

Wing-Comdr Beauman then wrote that the subject seemed ripe for investigation on scientific lines. I wrote to support his suggestion, and since the letter recalls the stormy European scene which was the background to this discussion perhaps I may be forgiven for quoting in part: 'Difficult though the world situation is I feel that from the discussion of such irrelevant matters nothing but good can come. For instance, had there been an Abominable Snowman among the exhibits at the Big Game Exhibition in Berlin the visit of Lord Halifax would not have been given the undesirable prominence it has. I notice regretfully that the correspondence appears to be failing and that a zoologist has been afforded space to drive yet another nail into the coffin of our abominable friend having first poisoned him with another dose of Latin. Difficult though it is, the confounding of scientific sceptics is always desirable, and I commend the suggestion that a scientific expedition should be sent out. To further this an Abominable Snowman Committee, on the lines of the Mount Everest Committee, might be formed, drawn from the Alpine Club and the Natural History Museum.'

The correspondence then died, all those who were interested or who had any suggestions to make having had their say. The Aunt Sally put up by Mr Kaulback had been well thrown at but was still there. Many had tried their hand, some of the throws had been pretty wild, and in the end no one had found a foot to fit even one of those five sets of tracks which 'looked exactly as though made by bare-footed men'. The origin of the epithet 'abominable' had been explained, the fauna of the Himalaya well canvassed, and ascetics dragged reluctantly from their caves – but all in vain. Mr Smythe had then put up his own Aunt Sally only to demolish it himself, and when the dust caused by that operation had subsided we found ourselves with two more lots of tracks, in addition to Mr Kaulback's, with no apparent owners.

At that time I had an open mind on the subject with perhaps a slight 'conservative' bias. I should have had no difficulty in concealing my chagrin if the scientific sceptics had been confounded. I had discussed the thing with both 'Bhalu' and 'Foreign Sportsman' and agreed with them that the tracks they had seen were not to be explained away by shouting 'Bear'. The circularity of their tracks was a peculiar feature and in one way significant, for of course a foot so shaped would be ideal for travelling in snow. Bearing in mind that the thing we were looking for was not so much a brute beast as a primitive form of man I propounded to them a theory to fit these round tracks and was laughed at for my pains. Beavers, bees, ants and some birds are by no means devoid of constructive ability and we must credit our Snowman with glimmerings of sense. Why should he not have adapted a primitive form of snowshoe? Anyone who has been in country where snowshoes are worn will have seen such a shoe, perfectly round and about one foot across. Such an obvious and simple aid must have been thought of before wheels were known or even before tree trunks were used as rollers for shifting heavy weights. To the objection that since snowshoes are not known to natives of the Himalayan regions I am crediting the Snowman with more than his share of intelligence, my answer is that the people of the Himalaya seldom or never travel on or above the glaciers while the Snowman never travels anywhere else. Necessity, as has been remarked before, is the mother of invention.

To come now to some evidence of my own which to my mind clinches the matter or at the very least clearly shows that for some of these strange tracks an adequate explanation has yet to be found. In maintaining that we really do not know what made some of these tracks the reader will allow that no extravagant demand is being made upon his credulity. I trust neither Mr Kaulback, 'Bhalu', 'Foreign Sportsman', nor myself will be classed with such masters of mendacity as Baron Munchausen, De Rougemont, or Barrère, for example – the Barrère of whom Macaulay recorded that there may have been as great liars though he had never met with them or read them. It is sometimes easy, of course, to see that which one fervently expects to see or even to persuade others that you have seen it; but these witnesses I have called and others who, like myself, are completely dependent in their travels upon local porters, would as soon establish the existence of the Devil as the 'Abominable Snowman'. For these porters are superstitious to a degree, liable to fits of discouragement, moroseness or even panic at any strange sight or untoward happening, and should their employer encourage their superstitions by appearing to share them he would find himself checked and thwarted at every unlucky turn. No, if we cannot wholly believe these men we must at least acquit them of wishing to deceive either themselves or others.

On the way back from Mount Everest in 1938 the party split

up. Taking with me two Sherpas I climbed a peak in North Sikkim and then proceeded via Tangu to the Zemu glacier. At Tangu, where there is a rest-house, we fell in with a large party of German scientists, led by a Dr Ernst Schaefer, who were engaged in a very thorough examination of the fauna and flora and every other aspect of Sikkim. The party included every breed of scientist known to man: ornithologist, entomologist, zoologist, anthropologist, geologist and other 'ologists of whom I had never even heard. Here, if anywhere, was a team capable of clearing up any difficult problems. I took the anthropologist (an earnest, inquiring man) on one side and over a few glasses of *Kümmel* abjured him to spare no pains in solving the mystery of *Homo odiosus*, and begged him on no account to be put off by the zoologist, who would assuredly tell him that any unaccountable tracks he might see in the snow were not those of a 'Snowman', not even a 'Snark', but merely those of a bear.

On 8 July from a camp on the Zemu glacier we set out to make the first crossing of the Zemu Gap, a 19,000-foot Col between one of Kangchenjunga's southern satellite peaks and Simvu. The weather was thick, the snow soft. Photography was impossible. As we plodded up the long easy snow slope to the Col, crossing the debris of some huge recent avalanches, I noticed by our side a single track of footsteps which, in view of the weather conditions (daily rain and snow), could not have been more than a few days old. The tracks led up the glacier to the Col and then disappeared on some rocks on the Simvu side. I remember feeling rather peeved at the time to think that we had been forestalled by some other climber, and we craned our necks anxiously over the top to see whether the tracks continued down the south side, which was extremely steep. They did not, but on returning to Darjeeling, in order to make sure, I began making inquiries. Lunatics are fairly scarce and only a lunatic would go 'swanning' about alone on the Zemu glacier, and had anyone been there the fact would undoubtedly have been known at Darjeeling. To grasp the significance of this evidence it must be understood that it is almost inconceivable that the movements of any climbing party in Sikkim should remain unknown. Porters talk, and leaving aside the number of mountaineering journals and books, the evidence of the letters we have been discussing is enough to show that men who climb in the Himalaya, though they may be strong, are not often silent.

I found that the last visit to the Zemu Gap had been made by a Major John Hunt, to whom I wrote and from whom I had the following reply: 'I was in Darjeeling yesterday and had a talk with Renzing [one of the writer's Sherpas] about your crossing of the Zemu Gap. I went up to the Gap in November last year (1937) and you will be interested to hear the following. When we went up there were distinct tracks up the final slope on the Zemu side – I thought at the time that they were both up and down as the tracks were double. From the top, moreover, steps had been cut down the slope on the Talung side to where it ends in the ice cliff. I used them myself to examine the descent. At the time I presumed they were made by the German party (Grob, Schmaderer and Peider) whom we had met at Lachen and who had spent six weeks on the glacier before us. I have, however, just received a copy of their book from which it is clear that *they never went to the Gap at all*. What on earth is the explanation of these tracks? They might conceivably have been those of an animal – though most improbable at that time of year with the deep snow we had had – but for the steps cut down the Talung side. Was the Gap crossed earlier last year and by whom?'

To my mind the answer is obvious – by the 'Abominable Snowman'. The writer of this letter implies that this hitherto uncrossed pass was crossed by someone who forgot to mention the fact. No one who swallows that can afford to laugh at those who like myself believe in a more rational explanation. There are degrees of credulity. Major Hunt seems to believe in this anonymous mountaineer who crosses difficult passes single-handed and says nothing about it, but he would probably boggle at the simple and satisfactory explanation of the mysterious tracks which I offer. It is tempting to call the author of them the 'Zemu Gap Snowman'; and such a precise label is justified, for in this case we have two independent witnesses who at different times have seen the same tracks in the same locality. And if one witness is considered biased, the other is a quite impartial observer who has taken no part in the controversy and who for all I know may never have heard of an 'Abominable Snowman'.

This evidence has not been published before so that the scientists have not had the chance to put up candidates from amongst the fauna of Sikkim, which by now must be thoroughly well known. (Are there, by the way, any bears there?) But in the Zemu Gap case there were no tracks which could be attributed according to fancy to bears, snow leopards, otters or gigantic one-legged birds, but plain tracks of large boots. I do not insist upon the boots, because in soft snow it is not possible to distinguish the nail marks which would be proof incontrovertible, but at any rate there were no signs of toe or claw marks; and it is worth noting that my two porters never so much as mentioned the word 'mirka' or 'yeti' but accepted the prints, as I did, for human feet. In fact the first thought that occurred to us, subsequently to be found without foundation, was that one of Schaefer's party had preceded us. And even supposing the tracks were made by boots, as I admit both the Sherpas, myself and Major Hunt assumed, there is no reason why the maker of the tracks should not have picked up a discarded pair of climbing boots at the old German Base Camp (at the Green Lake on the Zemu glacier) for attempts on Kangchenjunga, where there was, when I saw it, an accumulation of junk of all sorts, the jetsam of several expeditions, and put them to their obvious use. I have hinted that the subject of our inquiry may not be quite so 'dumb' as we think, and we are not to assume that a Snowman has not wit enough to keep his feet dry if they happen to be the shape that fit into boots.

I am unwilling to produce a scale drawing of a Snowman or even number his hairs on the strength of a footprint, though the professors in their search for the 'missing link' are less unassuming. G. K. Chesterton has remarked on the loving care and skill bestowed by them on their building up of Pithecanthropus – a bit of skull there, a few teeth here, and a thighbone from somewhere else – until at last they produced a detailed drawing carefully shaded to show that the very hairs of his head were numbered. I merely affirm that tracks for which no adequate explanation is forthcoming (not forgetting the strange Rongbuk stone footprint) have been seen and will continue to be seen in various parts of the Himalaya, and until a worthier claimant is found we may as well attribute them to the 'Abominable Snowman'. And I think he would be a bold and in some ways an impious sceptic who after balancing the evidence does not decide to give him the benefit of the doubt.

❊ from *Mount Everest, 1938* (1948)

Count Henri
Russell | *Protection*

A sheep-skin sack must be taken, and when worn, the wool must be on the inside, lest a hungry wolf mistake the climber for a sheep.

❋ from *Ascensions solitaires aux Pyrénées* (1901)

C. L. *Inker* | *The Ascent of F#*

'You may remember,' bellowed a tanned and weatherbeaten voice from the most comfortable armchair.

We gathered round obediently, filled our briars, and prepared to listen. The speaker, we knew, brooked no inattention from his fellow-members of the Senior Morons Club. Nor, indeed, would we willingly have missed one of his tales of peril on the heights, for the name of P. Cator, the great mountaineer, is known from Pole to Pole. His mother was one, which explains his Polish first name, Prevàri.

'You may remember,' Cator went on less noisily when we were all settled and attentive, 'the expedition of '36, when F#, the most pointed peak in the Himalaya, bowed its hitherto inviolate summit beneath the conquering boots of more than superhuman endeavour.'

We recognized this as a phrase from his latest book and nodded reverently. The great man leaned forward impressively.

'That summit, gentlemen, has in reality *never been trodden by the foot of man.*'

His voice was calm and cool, but there was an undeniable tension in the atmosphere. In the brief silence that followed his amazing revelation a waistcoat-button, which flew off under some emotional stress, sounded loud as a gunshot as it landed in a remote corner of the smoking-room.

'Tonight,' Cator went on, 'you shall hear the true facts – facts never before related to an eager world.'

He took a piton from his pocket and threw it with nonchalant accuracy at a surreptitiously dozing member before proceeding with his narrative.

'As you all know, my trusted companion Major R. O. Adahead and I started to traverse the foothills of the Himalaya in the Spring of '36. We reached the Pushbar Toopen, and in those barren hills recruited our little force of 700 porters from among the hardy Gaitas, toughest of hill-men. Then we travelled on, Adahead riding on a *yak* and myself on a *hak* which I had purchased for a couple of *laks*.

'After a journey fraught with mosquitoes and indigestion – the latter owing to a native food suggestively called *bhang* – we passed Nsil, the last outpost of civilization, and saw before us our goal. High into the firmament rose the giant spire of F♯, or, to give it its native name, Chomo-bungho-ma, which signifies 'the-Goddess-Mother-with-No-Room-On-Top'. At this point disaster overtook us. The porters deserted in a body and a cloud of dust. Although we had reduced each man's load to 300 pounds, and promised them a wage of 2*d*. per day as soon as our Post-War Credits were paid, they evinced dissatisfaction and left us.

'Adahead and I were alone. We had reached the terminus of a glacier, but it was moving in the opposite direction to that in which we wished to go. Had there been a monastery handy we might have ridden farther on *lamas*; but the monastery had been taken away as a souvenir by an American expedition in '35. I got out the map and Adahead produced his Wolf Cub Compass, Not a Toy. With their aid we discovered that we were on the Rhong Glacier.'

He paused as though expecting comment, but none came; if one excepts a resounding snore from a well-dined member. The mountaineer prodded him awake with the gnarled ice-axe which never left his side and resumed his enthralling tale.

'I will not weary you with an account of our many trials and mishaps. How we lived by shooting the agile *séracs* as they leapt from *bouquetin* to *bouquetin*; how I nursed Adahead through a bad attack of chilblains; how we were stung by Abominable Snowmen; how, in the face of literally incredible difficulties, we succeeded at last in pitching our series of camps on the mountain, calling our first one Camp A and so rendering obsolete the old system of numerical nomenclature – all these things you may read in my book *Summit Up*, now reprinted at 45*s*. On these things, then, I will not dwell, but take you at once to a morning at our highest camp, Camp T.

'All the gale-racked night I had tossed uncomfortably on Adahead, who was getting bonier every day on account of our reduced rations. But in spite of discomfort we were up early, ready and keen to make a dash for the summit. We could see it plainly, only 500 feet above us now, a needle-like pinnacle of dazzling white.'

He paused for a moment, a faraway look, both reminiscent and regretful, in his eyes. Either it was the Club port or the memory of that challenging summit. We decided it was probably the latter.

Young Meeter, the poet, dared to break that pregnant silence.
'The air
Up there
Is rare?' he inquired.
Cator glaciated him with a glance.

'The atmosphere at 28,000 feet, sir, is so rare as to be infrequent. We had to take sixty-five breaths at every step. This made it difficult for Adahead, who had failed his School Certif. in Maths and kept losing count. To make matters worse, the delays of our journey had brought us perilously close to the Monsoon. It might break at any moment. We pressed on into the frightful wind – on and up. By noon we had reached the foot of the final pyramid – or, rather, spike.

'Well indeed had our peak been named. The summit-cone was nothing but a thin spire of ice a hundred feet high. Such a problem had never been faced by mountaineers before. Adahead was fully occupied with his counting, for by now we were taking ninety-six breaths to a step. On me fell the burden of decision. What was to be done?

'It was the very thin-ness of that slender pinnacle that gave me the solution. With Adahead belaying our 120-foot rope I rapidly cut steps completely round the foot of the cone. You see my plan? It was to *walk* up that spire as a South Sea islander walks up a coconut palm, shifting the now complete circle of rope as I mounted. But it was not to be. Even as I rejoined Adahead he pointed with trembling finger to southward. The Monsoon was bending its way across the heavens – it was visibly about to break. And we could do nothing to strengthen it.'

He paused. The suspense was telling on us, and we mopped our sweating brows. A few weaklings called for double brandies.

'Quicker than thought I whipped out my knife and cut the rope.'

'Nearer and nearer,' continued Cator tensely, 'and still nearer came the Monsoon. Its hot breath fanned our cheeks. Then, with a tremendous report, it broke. Like an echo came a loud crack from the mountain on which we stood. The summit-pinnacle was toppling – yes, it was breaking clean off, weakened by the circle of steps I had cut in its base. Quicker than thought I whipped out my knife and cut the rope. Adahead did the same. We were not a second too soon. With a sickening plunge the whole summit of F♯ slid off the mountain to career down for 10,000 feet to the Wright Glacier on the east. At the same instant Adahead and I, with a plunge scarcely less emetic, slid down the frightful slopes on to the Rhong Glacier on the west.

'By some miracle we slid into Camp A unhurt save for a fractured whisky-flask. Our hopes, alas! were also shattered. The Monsoon was breaking into a thousand pieces all around us. Within the week we were heading for the foothills, our supplies of nourishment so nearly exhausted that we had to take water with it. You may judge of our joy when at last we reached the first sign of civilization – a finger-post bearing the simple legend To Nsil.

'And that, gentlemen, is the true story of that ill-fated expedition of '36. That is why the summit of F♯, that queen of virgin peaks, remains untrodden. For though we searched the Wright Glacier for the fallen summit, in order to set foot upon it, it was – naturally – inaccessible.'

'Why?' we all demanded.

'The Monsoon,' replied Cator sadly, 'had melted it.'

❀ from *Journal of the Midland Association of Mountaineers* (1946)

George | *Guides'*
Wherry | *Feet*

Returning to the Monte Rosa Hotel for a rest, I was fortunate in falling in with Captain Abney, who kindly photographed for me the naked feet of my guides in the act of climbing a rock. It has often been noticed that a guide can go face forward, and whole-footed up a slope, while the amateur following, and coming to the steep part, has to go on his toes or turn sideways. It seems possible that the angle made by the foot with the leg may be more acute in the guide who has climbed from infancy, and though it is probably very much a matter of balance, I wished to compare photographs of amateurs' feet when put into similar action.

❀ from *Alpine Notes and the Climbing Foot* (1896)

Ian
McNaught Davis

Mac the Belly
Talks to
Cassius Bonafide

The problems facing expedition leaders grow more acute every year as budgets soar and commercial pressures increase. Here in a fictitious conversation a bloated climbing commentator and TV star discusses the problems with a successful expedition leader.

MAC: *How did it all start, Cass?*
CASSIUS: Well, you see, Mac, I wanted to lead an expedition to the hardest small peak in the world. A new trial to test my developing personality.

You'd need a strong team for that.

Yes. I chose three of my very closest friends and we formed the hardest team of climbers in the world.

Sounds good.

Ah. That's when the problems start. Low peak – low box office. Nobody buys lousy routes on small peaks. We really needed a bigger scene. That's when I thought about Annaplus, the biggest and hardest face in the world.

But that would cost real money.

We estimated about £500,000 including oxygen and larks' tongues for the porters. A hundred thousand of rope and twenty thousand man days of margarine.

A hundred thousand feet, that's impressive.

Yards, old boy, yards.

Where did you get the cash?

Nobody is interested in cheap, trashy peaks. Annaplus isn't the highest but its face is the hardest in the world and by the time we were finished we believed it was the highest. You see it's a marketing problem, old boy. In the professional climbing world we call it creative mountaineering marketing. You find the mountain, create the image, sell like hell and then go out and climb it. If you get all this right, money falls on you like snow on the north face of Annaplus. We created the hardest route in the world on Annaplus, and who can resist that?

But it would take more than four of you?

Yes, that was a problem. In fact we ended up with eighty-six.

That includes the porters?

No. There were 16,000 of them, in fact the whole of the working population of the country. We had ten cameramen, four announcers, six producers, eight sound men, six lighting specialists, six camp managers, one for each camp, my English, American and European agents and forty-one climbers and a partridge in a pear tree.

That seems quite a change from four close friends.

Yes, I agree, but we were the hardest group of climbers ever to leave Britain; in fact none were left. They were all close loyal friends. We did have one American who's the hardest climber in the States and also the most religious. The idea came from my agent and it guaranteed the American sales of my book and implicitly got God into the team at the same time.

I'm impressed, Cass. How did the climb go?

We were fantastically successful. It took nine months to climb the first 500 feet. Harder than the North Face of the Eiger. Then two of the hardest men pushed through the next 8,000 feet to the summit. Artificial climbing all the way on overhanging ice with constant avalanches. It took them nearly all day. On the summit their anoraks were whipped by 200-mile-an-hour winds as they ate their margarine sandwiches.

You must have felt proud. Did the other thirty-nine go up as well?

No. They crapped out lower down, but don't quote me on that or I'll get my agent on to you.

Didn't they set everything up for the two you had chosen to go to the top?

We couldn't get all forty to the top, and if we hadn't got anybody we would have had no film, book or road-show. Think what that would have meant. So I think my plan was justified.

Don't you think in the future everyone will want a chance to go to the top?

Ha! ha! A few weeks carrying 80 lb. at 24,000 soon cools their enthusiasm and lets the hard men get through. Anyway it would be too expensive and bad box office. How can it be the hardest climb in the world if everybody gets up it? They'll think it's a scramble like Everest.

Tell me about your reputed craving for margarine at high altitude.

That's a bit below the belt, old boy. Marvellous stuff, spreads in 90 below and tastes like butter. We didn't take any. At least I don't think we did. You see I can't tell the difference.

What's next? Anything must seem dull after your last tremendous achievement.

This year's hardest climb in the world is the South Face of Everest. Great box office. An international team from ninety countries, 200 climbers. It's the Grand Slam. They are going to climb it by every route and they've got world-wide rights for film, books and this time it's covered by the BBC, not crummy old ITV, who didn't like to move out of base camp. It's fantastic.

Are you going, Cass?

I was asked but decided not to go. You see, old man, the whole thing is getting a bit too commercialized for me.

✻ from *Mountain* (1971)

W. E. Bowman | The Plan

After three hectic months of preparation we met in London, on the eve of our departure, for a final review of our plans. Only Jungle, who was to have spoken on the use of the radio gear and his own methods of route-finding, was absent. He rang up to say that he had taken the wrong bus and was not quite certain of his whereabouts; but he had just caught sight of the North Star and expected to join us shortly.

Burley, although not at his best – he told me he was suffering from London lassitude – gave us a detailed picture of the transportation arrangements. The object of the expedition was to place two men on the summit of Rum Doodle. This necessitated the establishment of a camp at 39,000 feet stocked with a fortnight's supplies for two, so that in the event of adverse weather conditions the party could wait in comfort for an improvement. The equipment for this camp had to be carried from the railhead at Chaikhosi, a distance of five hundred miles. Five porters would be needed for this. Two porters would be needed to carry the food for these five, and another would carry the food for these two. His food would be carried by a boy. The boy would carry his own food. The first supporting party would be established at 38,000 feet, also with a fortnight's supplies, which necessitated another eight porters and a boy. In all, to transport tents and equipment, food, radio, scientific and photographic gear, personal effects, and so on, three thousand porters and three hundred and seventy-five boys would be required.

At this point the telephone bell rang. It was Jungle, who seemed in the best of spirits. He had, he said, definitely identified his whereabouts as Cockfosters. We congratulated him and said we would expect him shortly.

Burley was congratulated on his masterly command of detail, although Wish expressed the opinion that the weight allowed for scientific equipment was scandalously small. He particularly wanted to take a mechanical glacier shovel and a three-ton pneumatic geologist's hammer, but neither of these indispensable items was allowed for. Burley was quite short with him. He pointed out that shovelling ice on Rum Doodle was quite a different thing from shovelling ice on Mont Blanc, while the rarefied atmosphere obtaining on the mountain would probably render the pneumatic gear impracticable. Wish burst into tears and said that he might as well go home at once, as he did not seem to be appreciated. Constant, in his tactful way, said that he was sure that Burley had no intention of belittling Wish's importance to the expedition; he had only meant that scientific gear was out of place on an expedition whose sole object was to place two men on the summit of Rum Doodle. This brought in Shute, who said he very much regretted the implication that scientific gear was a white elephant; one of the most important parts of our work would be the investigation of the effects of rarefied atmosphere upon three-dimensional colour television. Prone, who was suffering from a severe cold in the head, muttered something, which nobody quite understood, about 'ibportant bedical baterial' in a kind of enraged mumble.

Responsive, as a good leader should be, to human atmosphere, I sensed a hidden discord, and I quietly reminded all of the words of Totter: Mont Blanc might be climbed by a disunited party, Rum Doodle, never. This sobering thought had the desired effect, helped perhaps by the fact that Burley, overcome by London lassitude, had fallen asleep. Wish, who was to share a tent with him, was much distressed to find that he snored heavily, but he was consoled by Shute, who reminded him that owing to the attenuation of sound waves in a rarefied atmosphere the snores would be much less offensive at high altitudes.

Wish then outlined the scientific programme. In addition to investigations into the hypographical and topnological fossiferation of the area he hoped to collect new data on the effect of biochronical disastrification of the geneospherical pandiculae on the exegesis of Wharton's warple. He also hoped to bring back a pair of each species of living creature found on the mountain in order to study the possibility of breeding mountaineers capable of living normal lives at high altitudes.

At this point Jungle rang again. It was not Cockfosters, he

Shute described the photographic apparatus.

said, but Richmond. He had seen Cockfosters on a bus, but it turned out that the bus was *going* to Cockfosters. Owing to this he had, of course, set off in the wrong direction, but would be with us shortly.

After this, Shute described the photographic apparatus, the chief of which was a three-dimensional colour cinematographic camera. He hoped to obtain a film record of every aspect of the expedition's work. Suitable love-interest and accident sequences would be added by the company who had supplied the apparatus, and, with a patriotic song incorporated and the original material cut down to a minimum, the film was to be marketed on a world-wide basis as an epic of British heroism. If the summit were reached the successful pair would, if photogenic and under sixty, be offered film contracts for a picture entitled 'Tarzan and the Atrocious Snowmen'.

At this point a telegram was delivered. It read: SIGHTED BARKING CREEK NINETEEN THIRTY HOURS COURSE WEST NORTH

WEST EXPECT SHORTLY WEATHER COLD BUT FINE JUNGLE. The postmark was Hounslow.

Burley awoke with a complicated gurgle and said that it was all wrong to clutter up a climbing expedition, the object of which was to place two men on the summit of Rum Doodle, with a lot of scientific rubbish. He expressed the opinion that a scientist on an expedition was even more of a nuisance than his gear, which was considerable. He told us about his friend Groag, who shared a tent with a scientist on the 1923 expedition to Tum Teedle. Like all scientists, this one was very absent-minded. One day he inadvertently made tea with copper-sulphate solution instead of water, with the result that he and Groag turned blue and were colour-blind for a fortnight, being unable to distinguish blue from white. One day this scientist stepped off the edge of a snowfield, thinking the blue sky beyond a continuation of the snow. He was saved only by great effort and devotion on the part of Burley, who had the misfortune to be roped to him. Burley said that any ordinary man would have left him to his fate.

Wish said that he did not believe one word of the story. He himself had drunk gallons of copper-sulphate tea with impunity. The blue effect was no doubt due to cardiosynthesis of the bloodstream due to the rarefied atmosphere. He strongly resented the statement that all scientists were absent-minded.

At this point a knock was heard on the door. It was a sergeant from the local police station. A policeman in Lewisham had discovered a furtive stranger loitering near the gas works. He had been found to be in possession of maps and navigating instruments and had been arrested as a spy. He had given his name as Forest and this address as a reference. We gave the necessary assurances and asked the sergeant to transmit a message to the effect that we expected to see Jungle shortly.

Constant then told us about Yogistan, the country through which we must travel to reach the mountain. The natives, he said, were sturdy, independent people, friendly and of imperturbable dignity and cheerfulness. Their language, of which he had made a special study, was a branch of the aneroid-megalithic tongue. It contained no verbs and was spoken entirely from the stomach.

Prone said this was nonsense; if they spoke entirely from their stomachs they would suffer from permanent gastritis. Constant said that this was, in fact, the national disease, being hypodermic in ninety-five per cent of the population. Prone said that if this was the case he didn't see how they could keep cheerful. Constant said that this was due to their strength of character. He said that he was not used to having his word doubted, and if Prone persisted in his present uncooperative attitude he, Constant, would have to issue an ultimatum.

Prone then spoke to us about the problem of maintaining the fitness which was so essential to our success. He urged us to follow rigidly the precautions which he had laid down, and handed each of us several pages of closely typed manuscript. He said that if we followed his advice he could guarantee immunity from illness. Here he broke down with a fit of coughing and had to be thumped on the back. Constant did the thumping, and my impression was that he thumped a good deal harder than was strictly necessary. At any rate, Prone struck back at him, and a nasty incident might have ensued had not Prone been completely overcome by a fit of sneezing which made him quite incapable of defending himself.

I took this opportunity to thank all for their contributions, and remarked that I had no doubt that such little differences of opinion as might appear between us were evidence of the commendable frankness and openness with which we regarded one another, and that I had no reason to suppose that we would not make an efficient and united team. I reminded them of the words of Totter: In an expedition of this kind the desires of the individual must be subordinated to the common cause. Constant said Amen, and on this solemn note we woke Burley and set about making our preparations for the morrow's departure.

Next day we sailed from Tilbury. As I stepped aboard two telegrams were handed to me. One read: BEST OF LUCK REMEMBER NOT CLIMBING MONT BLANC TOTTER. The other ran: STRANDED ABERCWMSOSPANFACH WILL FOLLOW BY PLANE SEND HUNDRED POUNDS JUNGLE.

✻ from *The Ascent of Rum Doodle* (1956)

S. Russell Jones | # Cautionary Epigrams

FROSTBITE

Injections and dressings
Saved most of his nose.
He counted his blessings –
Six fingers, seven toes.

FREE CLIMBING

The use of a drill
On rock is depravity.
It takes Climber's Will
To overcome gravity
And not dentist's skill
To fill in a cavity.

OVERHANG

He scorned the thought of a fatal slip,
That cornice too had a curling lip . . .

ICECRAFT

So clever seemed Claude when he claimed to be clued
Up on seracs, his statements I scarcely pursued.
– Now I'm *not* like his icescrews but *properly* screwed.

AVALANCHE

In tumbled sheets of snow I try
To steal your warmth and seal our bond.
So cold, my love? O, tell me why –
Why do you not respond?

MUSEUM EXHIBIT

Douglas, Hudson, Croz and Hadow,
Firmly held by Whymper's spell,
Trusted this old rope whose shadow
Tolled the Zermatt passing bell.

EXHAUSTION

Snowbound sheep will creep in a rift and drift to sleep,
A sleep too deep to shift, a gift – if life is cheap.

SEARCH PARTY

'T-shirts and jeans will by now be quite white,
So blow on your whistles and flash a bright light,'
Said the Leader, then asked: 'Does anyone know
How to follow smooth sandal prints under new snow?'

MORE CAUTIONARY EPIGRAMS

If bagging all the Munros
Is only a duty one owes
To gods of fitness, God be witness,
From highland hills the fun goes.

*

A map has many uses, we are told.
It traces tracks and marks the bridges,
Defines the contour lines on ridges.
It will unfold, then tightly rolled
Can massacre the bloody midges.

*

When nursing a secret so *secret*
He hardly could hint or confess
That only he knew the location
And way to the Last Wilderness.
But willing to stir speculation
He wrote to the national press.
    No secret will stay long a secret
When known there's a secret to guess,
For guesswork promotes exploration;
Explorers blaze trails with their mess.
Then Chris, to your mortification,
Found – and lost – is your Last Wilderness.

*

Across the Styx a climber is ferried.
The dead man wasn't properly buried.

*

When days are hot and nights are cold
They work on icebound stones in combination,
So words like 'Rock' and 'Roll' may hold
In gully routes a lethal implication.

LINES ON A LOOSE PITON

On sloping stance some ropes will glance at me
And take a chance on safe advance. They see
No reasons to check my condition
Of rust from seasons' slow attrition,
But use me and abuse me, too sanguine to suspect
One day they well may pay for disrespect.

from *Climber and Rambler* (1983)

Robert Schultheis | *Chang*

These tall clay pots, each one holding at least twenty large kettles of chang, had been fermented especially for the party. Marpa's wife had strained them, and set aside one entire potful for Marpa, who filled his kettle again and again, drinking the kettle dry each time . . .

Eventually the holy Marpa drank so much chang that he fell unconscious out of his chair on to the floor, and had to be carried away to bed as the party went on . . .

– Description of a ninth-century drinking party hosted by Marpa the Translator, one of the founders of Tibetan Buddhism and now considered a deity in Tibet (Translation by Sonam Gyantse)

In a country where even the gods are drunk, you would expect the people to be heavy drinkers. You would be right. The Tibetan and the Nepali people are incredible alcoholics, in a class with the Russians, the Eskimos and the Ute Indians. Booze is everywhere in the Himalayas. Porters stop every hour to have a brew along the trail on a hot autumn day. Chai-house owners and farmers, huddled around a kerosene lamp, carry on rip-roaring, inebriated card games far into the night, and the shouting and laughter can be heard for miles. Whole alpine villages, men and women alike, wobble around like Bowery bums: bleary, yellow-eyed, grinning foolishly. Even Buddhist monks, chanting the holy texts at pujas, stop to wet their whistles from conveniently placed bottles of beer.

They drink chang, mostly – beer made (basically) by pouring boiling water over fermented millet, barley or rice, and letting the mix cool. As generations of Himalayan climbers have testified, chang is wonderful stuff at its best, the Pol Roger, the Château Rothschild of beers. At its worst, it is a dirty, thick, sour yellow gruel, with not enough alcohol in it to stone the bugs that swim merrily through it.

Wintering Bhotia nomads may live for months on an inebri-
ating porridge made from tsampa (roasted barley flour) and hot
chang – a delicious food, perfect on those subzero days in the
mountains when the wind howls down off the frozen peaks,
and the trail is closed by avalanches, and there is nothing to do
but sit in your black hide tent and spin yarn or sew up boots . . .

Rakshi, the other great drink of the Himalayas, is something
else entirely. Distilled from chang, toadstools, rotting wood and
anything else fermentable or distillable, it is volatile stuff,
producing temporary dementia, migraine headaches and hal-
lucinations, and turning mild-mannered porters into kukri-
wielding, homicidal maniacs. And it tastes awful – on a par
with French gin or Kachina peach brandy.

One night in the Himalayas of India, three years ago, I
foolishly drank five tall glasses of rakshi on top of two kettles of
chang, to celebrate the Dalai Lama's birthday. Late that night,
staggering home to my house in the jungle, shouting out
choruses of 'Pinball Wizard' and 'Bang a Gong' (Get It On), my
legs operating unsequentially, I stepped off the trail and free-
fell six feet into one of the streams of raw sewage that ran
through the village. In my drunken confusion it took me at least
ten minutes to extricate myself from the mess, crawling, falling
and cursing in the muck . . . By the time I clambered back up on
to the trail, I was soaking wet, hysterical with rage and adrenalin,
and the approximate odour of very old, very expensive cheese
– a lesson in moderation I will never forget, imprinted as it was
deep in my olfactory lobes . . .*

Why do they drink so much, these people of the Himalayas?
Well, you would too, probably, if you lived there: digging
potatoes or paddyfields out of rock-hard hillsides, humping
hundred-pound loads up and down high mountain passes,
sitting out the long, dark winters and the gloomy monsoons,
dodging the Smallpox Goddess, the Avalanche Demon and the
undodgeable devils of hard labour, chronic dysentry, leeches
and the rest . . .

* Li Po, perhaps the greatest poet in Chinese history, died in a somewhat
similar accident. Po, an enthusiastic drinker, was rolling home late one night
from the wineshop. He saw the moon's reflection in a canal by the road, reached
out to grab it, fell in and drowned.

I mean, the Himalayas are comparatively easy if you are a Sahibur Memsahib on vacation, trekking or mountaineering with a Sherpa, or perhaps a porter or two to porter your gear; your pockets stuffed with five- and ten-rupee notes; buying up every chicken, egg and glass of fresh buffalo milk within fifty miles. And, of course, you avoid the rainy season and the winter . . .

But to live there. A yak of a different hue.

Besides, as William James had noted: 'Sobriety diminishes, discriminates and says "no". Drunkenness expands, unites and says "yes". It is, in fact, the great exciter of the "yes" function in man . . .' Marpa, Milarepa, Saraha and the other famous beer-swigging Himalayan sages knew what they were about. And so, today, one runs into Tibetan caravaners – gloriously, hilariously drunk – leading their yak trains across the drifted snow of a high pass, whooping and shouting, one of them sawing away atonally on a single-string fiddle . . . They have style, the best of these high-altitude drunkards – a style approaching nirvanic

For thirty pence you can drink enough to fall off your bicycle ten times on the way back to Kathmandu.

grace in its absolute carelessness.* Chang fits into Himalayan life just as coca and lime fuel the tough, dogged existence of the Quechuas of the Andes.

The best chang in the Himalayas can be found right in the outskirts of Kathmandu, at the famous Bodnath Chang Shop, around the corner from Bodnath Stupa, that enormous, artificial concrete Himalaya which is one of the holiest places in Buddhism – and is, in fact, a bizarre and magical thing: a huge white-washed dome, rising like a snow peak out of a geometry of lesser domes and platforms and topped with a golden spire with eight eyes staring off into four directions. The overall effect is of something extra-terrestrial, or celestial, especially if one has just stepped out of a chang shop.

In the big, dark adobe rooms of the chang shop, one meets Tibetan traders, Newari artists (they are the master carvers and painters of Nepal), Limbu porters, Bhotia tramps, Western chang-freaks, all pouring down the lovely, pale stuff at fifty paise (about 2½p) a glass. Tall clay pots are stacked along the walls, chang in its various stages of fermentation: a drunkard's dream, indeed.

The Bodnath chang has a delicate, cidery taste, something like a cross between top quality applejack and a fine Moselle. For thirty pence, you can drink enough to fall off your bicycle ten times on the way back to Kathmandu. And if there is a better drink anywhere in the world, for anywhere near the same price, I would like to hear about it. (The only beer or wine that I have ever tasted that definitely was superior to Bodnath chang was a Bernkasteler Doktor Kabinett, and that cost me nineteen dollars for one bottle.

Chang is the stuff, all right, the drink of the gods, riding their snow clouds over Chogolisa, and as necessary to mountain life as the Silvretta binding, the riprap wall and the Moriarty hat.

❊ from *Mountain Gazette* (1976)

---

* This is summed up in the famous Tibetan saying, uttered before any dangerous endeavour to instil fearlessness: 'Everyone alive today will be dead in a hundred years.'